A Pocket Biography of Yeats

Gill Books
Hume Avenue, Park West, Dublin 12

www.gillbooks.ie

Gill Books is an imprint of M.H. Gill & Co.

Copyright © Teapot Press Ltd 2017

ISBN: 978-0-7171-7325-9

This book was created and produced by Teapot Press Ltd

Written by Fiona Biggs
Designed by Tony Potter & Alyssa Peacock

Printed in EU

This book is typeset in Garamond & Dax

A CIP catalogue record for this book is available
from the British Library.

5 4 3 2

A Pocket Biography of Yeats

Fiona Biggs

Gill Books

Contents

6   Introduction

12   Chapter 1: The Yeats Family

22   Chapter 2: The Early Years

32   Chapter 3: Education and Early Work

44   Chapter 4: Finding his Feet –
The Move Back to London

56   Chapter 5: A Lifelong Interest in the Occult

70   Chapter 6: The Pilgrim Soul – Maud Gonne

86   Chapter 7: Love and Marriage

102   Chapter 8: The Celtic Revival

116   Chapter 9: A Theatre for the Nation

130   Chapter 10: A Lasting Friendship – Lady Gregory

146   Chapter 11: The Land of Heart's Desire

158   Chapter 12: An Ideal Poor Man's House –
       Thoor Ballylee

172   Chapter 13: Romantic Ireland –
       Yeats and Nationalism

184   Chapter 14: Senator Yeats

196   Chapter 15: Eminence and Illness

214   Chapter 16: Dreams of Death

230   Chapter 17: Aftermath

240   Timeline of Yeats's Life and Works

250   Index to Poems Cited

255   Select Bibliography

256   Credits

Introduction

William Butler Yeats, poet, playwright, senator and Nobel laureate, Ireland's most famous literary son, was born in 1865, at the height of the Victorian era. His family belonged to the Anglo-Irish Protestant ascendancy, which was then on the brink of losing its privileged position in Ireland. His education was patchy and the fact that he achieved international recognition as a genius is largely due to his habit of reading widely and to his enquiring mind. This towering literary presence was, in an intellectual sense, a self-made man.

Yeats's somewhat unconventional and bohemian upbringing produced a shy and gauche young adult who found an outlet in writing. He met the old Fenian John O'Leary in 1885 and was encouraged by him to look

John O'Leary by John Butler Yeats

to the old tales and legends of Ireland as inspiration for his work. His early forays into writing – mostly plays – were just beginning to establish his reputation in Dublin, the city of his birth, when his father uprooted him in 1887 for one of the family's several moves to London. There, in literary circles that included Oscar Wilde, the young Yeats could have sunk into oblivion, but instead he rose to the challenge of his new milieu. He founded and joined societies, including the Rhymer's Club, which provided ground rules for writing verse that he carried through life. He had a lifelong fascination with the occult, and was a member of the fashionable Theosophical Society and the esoteric Hermetic Order of the Golden Dawn, the activities of which had a bearing on the direction of his poetry.

In 1889 Yeats met Maud Gonne for the first time and for many years he suffered the torments of unrequited love.

Gonne's influence on his life and poetry would be enormous. His attachment to her was such that he didn't contemplate marriage to anyone else until his late middle age. Yeats's great friend, patron and cultural collaborator, Lady Augusta Gregory, was keen for him to marry, in order that he would have a stable and supportive framework in which to write. Gregory even approved of his proposal to Maud Gonne's young daughter Iseult, believing that her youth would have made her easy to mould into the ideal poet's wife. Yeats eventually married Georgie Hyde Lees in October 1917, an auspicious time astrologically for such a union, according to Yeats's occult influences. The marriage produced two children and although it provided the stability he needed, his obsession with Maud had precluded the normal youthful affairs of the heart that might have been expected of a young man about town in London, and he sowed his wild oats at the other end of his life when he was an elderly married man.

Yeats loved Ireland and always made much of his Irishness. When the country was on the cusp of independence from Britain he committed himself to the emerging state, both politically and culturally. As a founder of the Irish Literary Revival he was pivotal to its success in reintroducing the population to its folkloric heritage, and together with Lady Gregory, he was a founder of the National Theatre (now the Abbey Theatre) and one of its directors. His youthful membership of the Young Ireland Society and the Irish Republican Brotherhood, encouraged by John O'Leary, led to his being appointed to the second house of the first Free State government in 1922. This, alongside his honorary academic distinctions and the award of the Nobel Prize for Literature in 1923, led him to declare 'I feel I have become a personage'.

When Yeats died in 1939 he had achieved international renown and was well on his way to becoming Ireland's favourite poet. Many of his poems have been learned by rote in Irish classrooms for decades, and the effect on the English language in Ireland is pervasive. The combination of odd juxtapositions and verses of hauntingly lyrical beauty remain embedded in the ageing memories of those who might, in the course of conversation, describe 'a terrible beauty', or say that 'the centre cannot hold'. However, W. B. Yeats's legacy is far more than his poetry – he was instrumental in bringing Irish culture and language back to life for the emerging nation.

CHAPTER 1

The Yeats Family

*Having
inherited a
vigorous mind
from my old
fathers*

William (Willie) Butler Yeats was born in Sandymount, Dublin, on 13 June 1865, the eldest child of John Butler Yeats and Susan Pollexfen. Ireland's most famous poet was a son of the Anglo-Irish Protestant ascendancy.

His father's family originated in Yorkshire, and had settled in Dublin towards the end of the 17th century. In the 18th century a Yeats married into the Butlers of Ormonde, and thereafter 'Butler' was retained as part of the family name. His mother's people, the Pollexfens, were a prosperous seafaring family who had moved from Cornwall to Sligo, where they ran a successful shipping business.

Yeats's grandfather (also William) was a clergyman, himself the son of a rector of the Church of Ireland whose parish was in Drumcliff, County Sligo, in the west of Ireland. Although William Butler Yeats Senior's own living was in the prosperous parish of Tullylish in County Down in the north of Ireland, he never felt at home in that part of the country and gravitated towards Sligo and Dublin, where he had been educated at Trinity College. Yeats's father, John Butler Yeats, was born on 16 March 1839 in Tullylish. He was, as were many sons of the Protestant clergy, intended for the church. It might have been expected that his first-hand experience of religion would have made him a devout conformist, but it seems to have had the opposite effect, leaving him with a deep scepticism for the irrationality of religion and all its trappings and a dislike of orthodoxy in any sphere. He once declared his belief that Christianity was 'mainly a myth of the frightened imagination'.

In 1862 John B. Yeats graduated from Trinity. His father died that year, leaving him a small estate which, managed properly, would have provided some

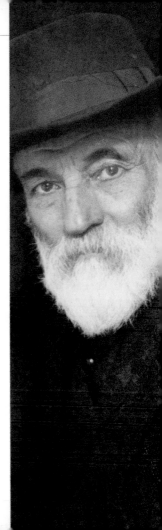

John Butler Yeats

measure of financial independence. In 1863, while still pursuing his legal studies, and after a very short courtship, John married Susan Mary Pollexfen, the quiet daughter of William and Elizabeth Pollexfen and the sister of his schoolfriends, Charles and George, through whom the couple met. The Pollexfens were Protestant unionists, a conservative and industrious mercantile family. They owned the Sligo Steam Navigation Company and were directors of the Sligo Gas, Light and Coke Company. It was perhaps a strange match for an unorthodox nationalist and it does not seem to have been made in heaven.

In 1866 John B. Yeats was called to the bar, a year after the birth of his famous son. He devilled for Home Ruler Isaac Butt, and with his good connections he could have had a successful career as a barrister. However, in 1867 he decided that his inclinations lay more in the artistic sphere and he abandoned the law for drawing and painting, enrolling in the Heatherley School of Fine Art in London for a course in painting. His early talent can be seen in a pencil drawing of his wife, entitled *Susan Yeats*, executed in 1867. Despite his ability, he would never make enough from his art to support his family.

The paternal decision to embark on the life of an artist plunged the Yeats family into a decade of travelling back and forth between London, Dublin and Sligo. William was born in Dublin, and it was here and in Sligo that Susan Pollexfen Yeats took refuge from London, a city that she hated and in which she never felt at home. She was quiet and introverted, her husband was a brilliant conversationalist with a wide acquaintance – the poet John Masefield said that he was 'one of the wittiest talkers of all time'. Susan is said to have had absolutely no interest in art (she famously never entered her husband's studio or attended an exhibition of his paintings). Increasingly, she found that she had to rely on her own family financially, since her husband's sudden career change didn't really accommodate the needs of a growing family. Young Susan (known in the family as 'Lily') was born in 1866, followed by Elizabeth (known as 'Lolly') in 1868. A son, Robert ('Robbie'), was born in 1870, and John ('Jack') made his appearance in 1871. Robert died in 1873. A sixth child, Jane, was born in 1875, but she didn't live to see her first birthday. Not unnaturally, Susan found the poor circumstances into which she had been thrust by her husband difficult to cope with. Her comfortable upbringing had not

prepared her for a life where she would have to undertake menial domestic tasks.

Between 1863 and 1873, John B. Yeats's income amounted to a paltry £10, awarded in 1863 as a prize at King's Inns where he was studying. (He used the money to visit his Pollexfen schoolmates in Sligo, and it was on this visit that he met his future wife.) His inherited estate was badly managed and the income it produced was not what he might have hoped for. At some point, he had started asking his in-laws for money, and his father-in-law sent cheques for relatively small amounts. It is clear from the correspondence between Susan and her husband that her family thought he had no common sense. He was probably relieved to be able to send his wife and children to stay in the family home in Sligo, the place Susan loved best of all – she was fascinated by the folk tales and legends told by the country people and would spend hours listening to local lore.

The first of the Pollexfen grandchildren were always welcome in Sligo, although William Pollexfen had a reputation for being somewhat irascible. Lily wrote in her memoir that 'Grandpapa

Pollexfen was liked, admired and avoided, he never talked to anyone, he grumbled, complained and ejaculated all day long, the past and the future had no interest for him at all, he was in such a state of irritation with the present moment that he could think of nothing else.'

In autumn 1874 John B. Yeats brought his family back to London to live in a small house in Earls Court. He was 35 and believed himself to be on the brink of a successful career as a painter. He was a gifted portraitist, but was very slow and meticulous and given to constant revisions of his work. There was never enough money – any income that he received from his mismanaged estate and his commissions disappeared almost without trace. He was 'perennially hopeful', always believing that fame and fortune were just around the corner, but they never arrived. He was a regular exhibitor at the Royal Academy and at the Royal Hibernian Academy, of which he became a member in 1892.

In 1875 the family moved to Bedford Park in Chiswick, a garden suburb (the first of its kind) designed to provide accommodation for writers and artists. John B. Yeats worked on portrait commissions and as an illustrator, but in 1880 the family moved back to Dublin, so that he could set up a portrait painter's studio there. In 1885 the Ashbourne Act allowed tenants to buy their landholdings from their landlords and he was able to sell his estate. He used the proceeds to move the family back to London in May 1887. Susan had a stroke later that year, followed by two more, and she remained an invalid until her death 12 years later.

In 1907, when he was 69, John B. Yeats moved to New York City, having travelled there with his daughter Lily on a visit. He refused to leave at the end of their stay and took lodgings in the city, where he soon became part of a community of writers, artists and intellectuals. He was popular socially, being an amusing raconteur – one of President Theodore Roosevelt's team said that he had 'introduced the art of conversation to New York'. He died on 3 February 1922 and is buried in Chestertown, New York.

CHAPTER 2

The Early Years

Life is a long preparation for something that never happens

By any standards, the poet's upbringing was unconventional. His parents had little in common and the family seems to have been endlessly on the move, from various locations in Dublin to various locations in London and to Sligo. The moves between one place and another were to further the father's career as a painter – in the Victorian era the mother's wishes or feelings would not have been taken into consideration. Susan Yeats lived most of her married life in inconvenient houses in cities she didn't like.

Yeats didn't have a particularly happy childhood. John B. Yeats was the most important influence in his young life, yet the young Yeats was diffident and seemed destined to disappoint his father in endless ways. He never learned to ride a horse, and when he was nine it was discovered that he was unable to read, no doubt as a result of parental neglect of his education rather than his own shortcomings. His father's reaction to this discovery was to threaten and coerce his son into learning his letters.

Yeats had a delicate constitution; his skin was unfashionably sallow and darkened easily when exposed to the sun. His mother's family were confounded that their eldest grandchild was physically weak and had no interest in or acumen for sporting activities. Much of his early childhood was spent with his mother and his siblings in Sligo, and his awkwardness and ineptitude must have made him particularly miserable when he was with his Pollexfen relatives. His aunts were concerned about his failure to thrive in any sense – his father liked to describe Susan's sisters as 'the dictatorial aunts', and believed them to have had a bad effect on his eldest son. Yeats's youngest surviving sibling, Jack, was favoured over the other Yeats children, perhaps because he was a happy and amusing child, his confidence in stark contrast to his older brother's shyness and diffidence.

Of the time he spent in Sligo, Yeats wrote: 'There was no reason for my unhappiness. Nobody was unkind, and my grandmother has still after so many years my gratitude and my reverence.' There is no mention of his grandfather here, although he once declared that 'I confused my grandfather with God, for I remember in one of my attacks of melancholy praying that he might punish me for my sins.'

The Pollexfens were conventionally religious, and although Yeats's father had no truck with religion, Susan took the children to church every Sunday. The young Yeats had a keen belief in God and was devout, although when he was nine or 10 his father refused to accompany the family to church, causing the youngster to question his own belief. However, the inability of some local farm workers to explain to him where calves came from led him to believe that it was a mystery that only God could understand, therefore God must exist. In his childish mind, the matter was settled.

The Pollexfen family house, Merville, was a large stone-built house dating from the late 18th century, set in an estate of 60 acres. There was a wonderful view of majestic Ben Bulben from its elegant windows, and the mountain would have provided a constant background to the young boy's life and thoughts. In 1938 he would write of the horsemen who 'ride the wintry dawn/Where Ben Bulben sets the scene'. Yeats took refuge from his unhappiness and uncertainty in the Sligo countryside, his love for which probably equalled that of his mother. He once said that it was 'the place that has really influenced my life the most'. Throughout his life he was always drawn there, coming back to it again and again in his poetry. He wandered through the countryside and explored the coastal caves, his mind mostly occupied with daydreams.

Although Yeats was shy and diffident with most of his older relatives, he had a good relationship with his siblings, especially Lily, who had great admiration for her big brother. All of the Yeats children took after their artistic father, as can be seen from the holiday drawings that they spent hours completing. Yeats, encouraged by his father, studied art for several years after leaving school, although it became clear that he had no outstanding talent, and Jack was the only one of that generation who would go on to achieve greatness as a painter.

Until he was nine years old, much of Yeats's time was spent in Sligo, but he then had two unbroken years in London. He wasn't sent to school until 1877, when he was 11, but in 1880

the family moved back to Ireland again, this time to Howth, in North County Dublin. The move pleased Yeats, who had not liked living in London, and he loved Ireland – he made much of his Irishness throughout his life.

His day-dreaming continued – he could never apply himself to any proper course of study as his concentration was poor. He later described his mental attitude to study as a form of psychological weakness. He sometimes slept in caves or in the lush gardens of Howth Castle, dreaming of himself as a master magician or poet who could achieve domination of the world simply by the power of his mind. His early interest in magic and the occult became a fascination that would stay with him throughout his life. In reality he was shy and awkward, but in his head he was a hero, like those of old. He had inherited his mother's love of folklore and began to collect local tales, some of which would appear in *The Celtic Twilight*, published in 1893.

While he wandered alone and mused in the Howth countryside, his thoughts turned to writing verse. His father had a great regard for poetry as an art form, believing it to be the highest form of literature, and was in the habit of reading aloud to his son the most passionate and colourful extracts from Shakespeare, Blake, Shelley and Rosetti. His son's first (unpublished) efforts were self-aware, wordy and slow, and they were very old-fashioned in their language, but they were a way for a lonely young man to express his feelings and experience a sense of power and usefulness. These early efforts enabled him to experiment with the mechanics of writing poetry, a process that provided the foundations for a fluency and lyricism that would stand him in good stead throughout his life.

Although Yeats's boyhood and youth were difficult and coloured with anxiety and a sense of inadequacy, in middle age he would look back on his childhood as a time of carefree innocence. His poem 'To a Child Dancing in the Wind' captures a sense of youthful optimism in just a few lines.

To a Child Dancing in the Wind

Dance there upon the shore;
What need have you to care
For wind or water's roar?
And tumble out your hair
That the salt drops have wet;
Being young you have not known
The fool's triumph, nor yet
Love lost as soon as won,
Nor the best labourer dead
And all the sheaves to bind.
What need have you to dread
The monstrous crying of the wind?

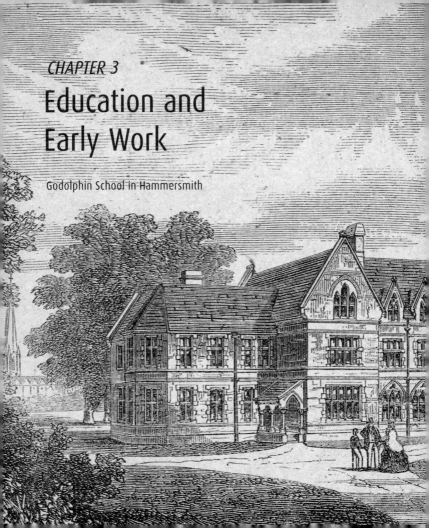

CHAPTER 3
Education and Early Work

Godolphin School in Hammersmith

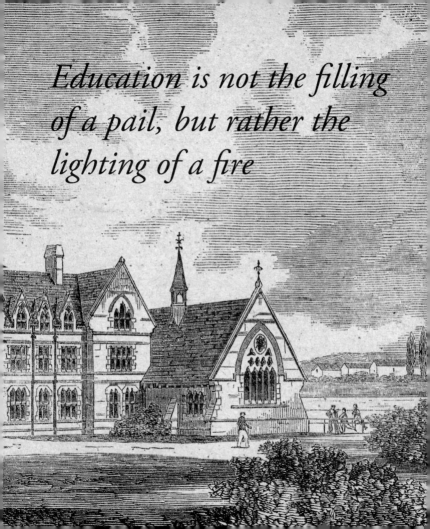

Education is not the filling of a pail, but rather the lighting of a fire

The breadth of language and subject matter in his work might give the impression that Yeats had received the solid education that was usual for boys in late Victorian middle-class circles. However, his schooling was at best patchy, and he was never a good student.

When Yeats was a small child his father put into practice a theory that was doing the rounds in some social circles at the time that educating children at too young an age was stifling and would impede their intellectual development. The conventional Pollexfens were, not surprisingly, disturbed by this avant-garde approach to the education of their grandchildren, but they seem to have had little say in the matter. John B. Yeats took over his eldest son's education when the boy was nine – he used to take him on instructive nature rambles through the countryside in Slough, which would have appealed to a boy so used to wandering alone in the beautiful Sligo countryside. His mother's contribution to the education process was to regale him with the Irish folk tales and legends that she knew and loved so well.

In 1877, when he was 11, it was decided to send him to the Godolphin School in Hammersmith. This first experience of formal schooling was not a success and Yeats didn't shine academically. He was laughed at and bullied because he was relatively poor and Irish and had no aptitude for games. That might have been acceptable if he had been a good student, but he was dreamy and inattentive and learned very little – a report said that Latin was his best subject, but described him as 'very poor in spelling' (his spelling and punctuation would be erratic throughout his life). The Godolphin School is now a well-regarded girls' school, but in Yeats's time it had little to recommend it. He himself said it had 'the rough manners of a cheap school', and he regarded its pupils as the sons of failures, an early expression of the sense of superiority that he carried with him throughout his life. He took refuge in his Irishness and focused his mind on those extra-curricular subjects that interested him, including myths, legends and the supernatural.

When the family returned to Dublin in 1880, they lived for a short time at Harold's Cross, later moving to Howth, a few miles north of Dublin city, and Yeats was enrolled as a pupil in

Dublin's Metropolitan School of Art, c.1905

the Erasmus Smith High School in Harcourt Street (now the High School, relocated to Rathgar) from 1881 to 1883, when he turned 18. The headmaster despaired of his lack of application – he was good at natural science subjects but poor at mathematics and the all-important classics. He seems to have been something of a disruptive influence in the school, failing to pay attention and distracting his classmates, and his teachers didn't hold out much hope for his future.

Always heavily influenced by his father, the schoolboy Yeats spent a lot of time in the painter's studio, which was not far from the school premises, absorbing the conversation and debate of the many artists and writers who frequented it. It is perhaps not surprising, then, that when he left school he decided not go to Trinity College Dublin as would have been expected of him, his lacklustre academic performance at school notwithstanding (he would have belonged to the third generation of Yeats men at Trinity). Encouraged by his father, he decided to study at the Metropolitan School of Art in Dublin, which he attended from 1884 to 1885, going on to the Royal Hibernian Academy School for several months in 1886. He was out of sync with the painting fashions of the times – he favoured the Pre-Raphaelites, while the Dublin art schools in the late 19th century were concentrating on the French Impressionists. Quite apart from his unfashionable preferences, it soon became clear that he had no great talent as a painter.

Although his formal education, limited as it was, had not been remarkable, Yeats had been expanding his mind. While still at school he had started writing poetry and plays – he admired Shelley and Edmund Spenser, and his early work was romantic, dreamy and heavily influenced by the world of the occult and the supernatural. His first works were written when he was only 17. Later in life he would dismiss them as 'not of any merit'. The early plays feature enchanting temptresses with supernatural powers – the themes of love and death would reappear in much of his work. His first play, *Vivien and Time* (1884), was performed by the playwright and some friends in a private house in Howth. A prefatory poem hints at the language and cadence of his more mature work:

I've built a dreaming palace
With stones from out the old
And singing days, within their graves
Now lying calm and cold.

A dramatic play in verse form, *Mosada*, another work from 1884, is described as a 'verse play in three scenes' and was published in 1886 in the recently founded *Dublin University Review*. Although the limited run of 100 copies was paid for by his father (the frontispiece is John Butler Yeats's touching portrait of his son, which conveys all his youthful uncertainty and awkwardness), it must have given the young author a thrill to see his work in print. The play involves a Moorish enchantress, the Inquisition and love inadvertently betrayed. Although most critics were unimpressed, Yeats's friend, the novelist and poet Katharine Tynan, later described it as 'wonderfully clear, rich and soft in its minor tones', creating a beauty that was 'rapt and exalted, the very spirit of poetry'.

Love and Death was his third dramatic effort of 1884 and it was based on one of his father's Pre-Raphaelite designs. In 1915 he summarised it in *Reveries over Childhood and Youth*.

A king's daughter [Ginevra] loves a god seen in the
luminous sky above her garden in childhood, and to
be worthy of him, and put away mortality, becomes
without pity and commits crimes, and at last, having
made her way to the throne by murder, awaits [his
coming] among her courtiers. One by one, they
become chilly and drop dead, for, unseen by all but
her, her god is walking through the hall. At last, he is
at her throne's foot, and she, her mind in the garden
once again, dies babbling like a child.

The play borrows heavily from Yeats's literary heroes –
Edmund Spenser, Shelley, Keats, William Morris, the Pre-
Raphaelites – and had all the hallmarks of a teenage author who
spent a great deal of time alone with his imagination. However,
it also gives us a glimpse of the poet he would become.

I see the company of timid ghosts
At evening also when the sun is low
Each with its finger to its lips goes by
Poor wild unutterable mysteries.

One of the first poems Yeats ever published (in 1885) was extracted from the play and given its title:

> Go ask the springing flowers,
> And the flowing air above,
> What are the twin-born waters,
> And they'll answer Death and Love.

The final play of that prolific year was *The Island of Statues, An Arcadian Fairy Tale* – the title and subtitle give the gist of the subject matter. The epilogue, presented in verse, gives an insight into the 18-year-old's views on the importance of literature and the value of the 'word':

> The woods of Arcady are dead,
> And over is their antique joy;
> Of old the world on dreaming fed;
> Grey Truth is now her painted toy;
> But O, sick children of the world,
> Of all the many changing things
> In dreary dancing past us whirled,
> To the old cracked tune that Chronos sings,
> Words alone are certain good.

41

In 1886 Yeats decided to give up the study of art for good, in defiance of his father's wishes. His early attempts at writing plays and poetry, perhaps even the action of putting words on paper, must have bolstered his own opinion of his abilities and provided him with the self-confidence to pursue a career as a writer.

In 1885 Yeats had met the returned exile and patriot John O'Leary. Under his influence he joined the Young Ireland Society and also the Contemporary Club, an association of nationalist intellectuals, which encouraged him to mine the rich seam of Irish stories and ballads for his poetry, rather than relying on the mystical and romantic themes that he had been concentrating on. The Victorian public preferred poetry that dealt with romantic themes and heroes of old, and to go in another, Irish, direction, was a bold move, but it was in line with the nationalism he had inherited from his father. His first Irish poem, 'The Two Titans, a Political Poem', was published in 1886. It is considered to have little merit, but its importance lies in the shift it represents. Yeats later said, in a note to his *Collected Works in Verse and Prose*, published in 1908, 'When I first wrote I went here and there for my subjects as my reading led me, and preferred to all other countries Arcadia and the India of romance, but presently I convinced myself […] that I should never go for the scenery of a poem to any country but my own, and I think that I shall hold that conviction to the end.'

John O'Leary (1830–1907), journalist. Animated sketch done on the spot by John Butler Yeats in 1886.

CHAPTER 4

Finding his Feet – The Move Back to London

While I stand on the roadway or the pavements grey

In May 1887, just before his 22nd birthday, Yeats had to move back to London with his family. It was not a good time for him to leave Dublin, where he was just beginning to make his mark, but without any means of supporting himself he was still tied to the family unit. In the larger literary pond of London he felt displaced and invisible. He had published only in Dublin and his lack of formal education put him at a disadvantage. He mixed in the intellectual and artistic circles of the day, but felt out of place, gauche and awkward. He often managed to escape to his uncle George Pollexfen's house in Sligo, which must have given him some breathing space.

Living in poverty and obscurity with his family in Earls Court gave rise to 'dreadful despondent moods'. His mother suffered three debilitating strokes not long after the move to London and lived the sad and isolated life of a permanent invalid for the rest of her days. His father had descended into gloom, and Yeats could not find in himself any enthusiasm for writing poetry. He turned instead to writing criticism and found something of a niche for the time being.

His father, resigned to his son's change of career focus, worried that he would stop writing creatively altogether and he encouraged him to write stories if he could not write poetry. He complied by writing a couple of semi-autobiographical stories. The first, *Dhoya*, is full of magic symbolism and Yeats contrives a bad end for the hero of the tale. John B. Yeats urged him to write instead about 'real' people – the result was *John Sherman*, which was a tale about a 'real' person who had no interactions with the fairy world.

Walsh's Royal Mail and Day Car, Sligo, c.1885

In 1889, with the help of John O'Leary, who was very encouraging to young Irish writers and poets, he published his first major poetic work, 'The Wanderings of Oisin', a long narrative poem in three parts that demonstrates both his growing ability and increasing confidence as a poet.

Yeats was an enthusiastic founder and joiner of clubs and societies in which he could pursue his many interests. He threw himself into their activities and always became involved in the internal politics. In 1890 he founded a poetry collective called the Rhymers' Club with Ernest Rhys, who later became the editor of Everyman's Library. The final group consisted of 14 members, including T. W. Rolleston and Edwin Ellis. Non-members (as was common in societies in those days women could not attend under any circumstances) could come

Image from *Myths and Legends: the Celtic race* (1910), T.W. Rolleston to meetings – an illustrious visitor was Oscar Wilde, then at the height of his career. The club met monthly for dinner at Ye Olde Cheshire Cheese pub in Fleet Street – after dinner they repaired to an upstairs room for readings of their own works and debates about poetry. The members soon became known as the Decadents. With the benefit of hindsight Yeats would later refer to the membership of the club as a 'tragic generation' who were obsessive about obeying the rules, although throughout his life he complied with their insistence on 'rhythm and cadence … form and style' as the essential stock-in-trade of any poet. In 'The Grey Rock' (1916) he addresses those poets 'with whom I learned my trade/Companions of the Cheshire Cheese':

> You kept the Muses' sterner laws,
> And unrepenting faced your ends,
> And therefore earned the right – and yet
> Dowson and Johnson most I praise –
> To troop with those the world's forgot,
> And copy their proud steady gaze.

At this time, under the influence of the Rhymers, his verse output was almost exclusively love poetry. 'Ephemera' is an example of his somewhat resigned and world-weary work at this point, written when he was 24. It must be borne in mind that Yeats didn't have a sexual relationship until he was 30. However, in 1889 he had met Maud Gonne for the first time, sparking an unrequited passion that lasted for almost 30 years, giving rise to a great deal of love-lorn verse.

> 'Your eyes that once were never weary of mine
> Are bowed in sorrow under pendulous lids,
> Because our love is waning.'

>   And then she:
> 'Although our love is waning, let us stand
> By the lone border of the lake once more,
> Together in that hour of gentleness
> When the poor tired child, Passion, falls asleep.
> How far away the stars seem, and how far
> Is our first kiss, and ah, how old my heart!'

Pensive they paced along the faded leaves,
While slowly he whose hand held hers replied:
'Passion has often worn our wandering hearts.'

The woods were round them, and the yellow leaves
Fell like faint meteors in the gloom, and once
A rabbit old and lame limped down the path;
Autumn was over him: and now they stood
On the lone border of the lake once more:
Turning, he saw that she had thrust dead leaves
Gathered in silence, dewy as her eyes,
In bosom and hair.

        'Ah, do not mourn,' he said,
'That we are tired, for other loves await us;
Hate on and love through unrepining hours.
Before us lies eternity; our souls
Are love, and a continual farewell.'

By the end of the 1890s, his love poetry was more
immediate, with a lighter, more lyrical touch, and much of it
seems more memorable because it is easy to commit to memory.

He Wishes for the Cloths of Heaven

Had I the heavens' embroidered cloths,
Enwrought with golden and silver light,
The blue and the dim and the dark cloths
Of night and light and the half-light.
I would spread the cloths under your feet:
But I, being poor, have only my dreams;
I have spread my dreams under your feet;
Tread softly because you tread on my dreams.

By this time, Yeats had transformed himself from the shy, untidily dressed, bearded fledgling poet who had come, very reluctantly, to London in 1887. By 1889, he had shaved his beard and was sporting a moustache instead. In November 1893, Katharine Tynan wrote in *The Sketch* that when she had known him in Dublin,

> He was as untidy as a genius newly come from the backwoods. He used to affect scarlet ties, which lit up his olive face. They were tied most carelessly. Ordinary young men who had been at school with him and resented his being a genius, used to say that the carelessness was the result of long effort; but one never believed them. Now he wears the regulation, London costume, plus a soft hat, and his ties are dark silk, knotted in a soft bow.

This was the year in which Yeats published his accomplished 'The Lake Isle of Innisfree', one of the most quoted poems from the early period of his work.

I will arise and go now, and go to Innisfree,
And a small cabin build there, of clay and wattles made:
Nine bean-rows will I have there, a hive for the honey-bee,
And live alone in the bee-loud glade.

And I shall have some peace there, for peace comes dropping slow,
Dropping from the veils of the morning to where the cricket sings;
There midnight's all a glimmer, and noon a purple glow,
And evening full of the linnet's wings.

I will arise and go now, for always night and day
I hear lake water lapping with low sounds by the shore;
While I stand on the roadway, or on the pavements grey,
I hear it in the deep heart's core.

By 1896 his facial hair had completely disappeared and he was dressing in black suits. He had become the clean-shaven, conventionally though artistically well-dressed young poet that we recognise from his father's 1898 portrait of him. As the century drew to a close his output as a critic, storywriter and poet had contributed to making him a well-known literary figure about town.

CHAPTER 5

A Lifelong Interest in the Occult

EXARP
HCOMA
NANTA
BITOM

The mystical life is the centre of all that I do

of Adept lies in Pastos. upon his back in
all Regalia. Complete Symbol on his breast
ing by Phœnix Collar. Arms crossed on
breast—not hiding Symbol—hands bear the
Scourge and Crook between them the Book I
of Pastos closed and Altar stands over its
fire. Second and Third Adept are outside
the Vault. Elemental Tablets and Kerubic
figures being outside the Door of the Vault.
Second' Associate Ad Min Let the Aspirant
be re-admitted. Third A opens door of Ros.
Admits Aspirant who bears Wand & Crux
ansata of the Chief Adept. Place Aspirant
in front of and facing door of Vault. Seated
cond = Before the Door of the Vault a, Symboli-
ansians of the threshold of the Entrance are the
elemental Tablets and Cherubic Emblems. We
before the Mystical Gate of Eden stood the
watchful Cherubim and the Sword of Flame.
These Cherubic Emblems are the Powers of the
Angel of the Tablets, Observe that the Circle
represents the four Angels bound together in
each tablet through the operation of the
all pervading spirit, While the Cross within, for

Yeats's interest in magic and the occult has been well documented – throughout his life he referred to the power of the spirit world in his work. His fascination probably began during childhood when he absorbed the myths and legends of Ireland that his mother related to the Yeats children. When he was enrolled at the Metropolitan School of Art he became acquainted with his fellow student George 'AE' Russell. Under his influence, and searching for an alternative to the dry Protestantism of his mother's family and the religious scepticism of his father, he immersed himself in a study of the occult.

Russell and Yeats were two of the founding members of the Dublin Hermetic Society, which met for the first time in a room in a Dublin back street on 16 June 1885. The society was established to further study of magic, mysticism and eastern religion; the members rejected the importance of science in favour of a belief in the power of the imagination. Although theosophy (a mixture of eastern mysticism and western science

1903 portrait of AE (George W. Russell) (1867–1935), Poet, by John Butler Yeats, 1839–1922

which maintains that all religions have a hidden sacred teaching and that a deeper spiritual reality than is apparent on the surface can be accessed through intuition, meditation or revelation) was gaining in popularity as a philosophy, Yeats and Russell were not convinced by it and neither of them joined the Dublin branch of the Theosophical Society, founded originally in New York by Helena Blavatsky and Henry Olcott. By the time the Yeats family moved to London in 1887, Madame Blavatsky was living there. When Yeats met her he was very taken with her. 'She made upon me an impression of generosity and indulgence,' he wrote.

In late 19th-century London spiritualism was in vogue and séances were relatively commonplace. Although Madame Blavatsky discouraged any dabbling in the occult,

Helena Blavatsky, 1844–1845

Yeats's interest was such that he went to a séance, accompanied by Katharine Tynan. Madame Blavatsky was persuaded by the interest in magic of some Theosophical Society members to set up the Esoteric Section (a secret section) of the society in 1888, with the aim of promoting 'a deeper study of esoteric philosophy'. Yeats was an enthusiastic early member of the new offshoot. Apart from channelling his interests and his developing beliefs about the very nature of being, it gave him a way of belonging in the new milieu of London society that had no connection with his family.

Yeats, however, was to be disappointed with the failure of the new offshoot section to carry out occult experiments. Although the members studied magical and esoteric symbols, practical magic was not countenanced. Some members, however, took it upon themselves to conduct some experiments (one was an attempt to raise the ghost of a flower, another to provoke a particular dream by placing a symbol under the sleeper's pillow), but these had no results, positive or otherwise. In 1890, Madame Blavatsky, possibly concerned that her society was being hijacked, asked Yeats to resign.

This may not have been a devastating development for him – just a few months earlier he had joined the Hermetic Students of the Golden Dawn, a smaller society that placed a lot of emphasis on occult rituals and had initiation ceremonies for each rank of the order. While the Theosophical Society concentrated on eastern wisdom, the Golden Dawn explored astrology and magic, thus appealing to Yeats.

His interest in the occult may seem strange to pragmatic, materialist 21st-century minds, but it was not uncommon in the late 19th century. Established literary men and scientists were also members of the Golden Dawn, as was George Pollexfen, Yeats's favourite uncle. For Yeats membership of the society was a crucial part of his spiritual quest – he believed strongly in the divine.

He was committed to the occult and to the Golden Dawn for the rest of his life, although it took a back seat when he became involved in establishing an Irish national theatre in the early years of the 20th century. By 1893, at the age of 28, he had achieved five of the order's 10 grades or ranks, taking a solemn oath to

keep secret all things connected with this Order and
its secret knowledge from the whole world … I will
from this day forward apply myself unto the GREAT
WORK which is to purify and exalt my spiritual
nature that with the Divine Aid I may at length
attain to be more than human, and thus gradually
raise and unite myself to my Magus and Divine
Genius, and that in this event I will not abuse the
great power entrusted to me.

In 1892 John O'Leary had expressed his concern that Yeats
was absorbed in his occult studies to an unhealthy extent. The
writer's response was cutting.

Yeats' hand-made
Pentacle, which
represents the element
of Earth. His magical
motto, Demon est Deus
Inversus, is painted on
the pentacle.

> It is ... absurd to hold me 'weak' ... because I choose to persist in a study which I decided deliberately four or five years ago to make next to my poetry, the more important pursuit of my life. ... The mystical life is the centre of all that I do and all that I think and all that I write.

His interest in the occult was part of his private life – the privacy was aided by the fact that the Golden Dawn was a very secret society. In his work as a poet, he knew that he needed to engage with the material aspects of the world – although he used occult symbolism (notably the rose) in some of his poems, he deliberately avoided concentrating too heavily on mysticism. In 1899 he published a collection called *The Wind Among the Reeds*, many of the poems in which used occult symbolism.

Front cover of *The Wind Among the Reeds*

The Secret Rose

Far-off, most secret, and inviolate Rose,
Enfold me in my hour of hours; where those
Who sought thee in the Holy Sepulchre,
Or in the wine-vat, dwell beyond the stir
And tumult of defeated dreams; and deep
Among pale eyelids, heavy with the sleep
Men have named beauty. Thy great leaves enfold
The ancient beards, the helms of ruby and gold
Of the crowned Magi; and the king whose eyes
Saw the Pierced Hands and Rood of elder rise
In Druid vapour and make the torches dim;
Till vain frenzy awoke and he died; and him
Who met Fand walking among flaming dew
By a grey shore where the wind never blew,
And lost the world and Emer for a kiss;

And him who drove the gods out of their liss,
And till a hundred morns had flowered red
Feasted, and wept the barrows of his dead;
And the proud dreaming king who flung the crown
And sorrow away, and calling bard and clown
Dwelt among wine-stained wanderers in deep woods;
And him who sold tillage, and house, and goods,
And sought through lands and islands numberless years,
Until he found, with laughter and with tears,
A woman of so shining loveliness
That men threshed corn at midnight by a tress,
A little stolen tress. I, too, await
The hour of thy great wind of love and hate.
When shall the stars be blown about the sky,
Like the sparks blown out of a smithy, and die?
Surely thine hour has come, thy great wind blows,
Far-off, most secret, and inviolate Rose.

Maud Gonne, for whom Yeats carried a torch for decades, was similarly fascinated by the occult. Yeats kept a notebook recording his and Gonne's occult experiences. They had a close spiritual connection and had committed to an 'astral marriage'; one morning in 1908 she wrote to him of a vision she had had: 'I had such a wonderful experience last night that I must know at once if it affected you & how? At a quarter of 11 last night I put on this body & thought strongly of you & desired to go to you.'

Yeats never rejected Christianity – he soon discovered that the Golden Dawn steered its members closer to Christianity as they rose through its ranks. In 1896 he conceived the idea of setting up a new form of Irish worship that would 'unite the radical truths of Christianity to those of a more ancient world'. He hoped that his occult practice would lead him to an intimate knowledge of a sacred Ireland and that the new religion would promote a sort of spiritual Irish nationalism. Together with several other students of the occult, including Maud Gonne (who had romantic ideas of Ireland as a sacred and magical land), he planned to revive ancient Druidic practices and intended to establish the revival at the 'Castle of Heroes' on an abandoned island in Lough Key, County Roscommon. The castle was never built, but for six years Yeats worked closely with the group, and with MacGregor Mathers, the founder of the Golden Dawn, on the planning of the rituals, symbolism and teachings that would define the new religion. The resources they used were Irish myths and legends, Golden Dawn teachings and their own 'astral' journeys, during which they travelled to a hidden Ireland and were able to access its sacred power.

Although all the planning came to nothing in terms of the establishment of the new order, Yeats's involvement with it played an important role in his setting up of an Irish national theatre. This enormous endeavour distracted him from his involvement in the Golden Dawn for the first decade of the 21st century, but his marriage, relatively late in life, brought about a renewed engagement with the occult – his wife, also a Golden Dawn member, was practised at automatic writing. The revelations they received helped them to order their life together, and they provided the basis for Yeats's huge philosophical work, *A Vision*, published in 1925.

CHAPTER 6

The Pilgrim Soul
– Maud Gonne

Maud Gonne

The troubling
of my life began

Maud Gonne was born on 21 December 1866 in Surrey, England, where her father was serving as an officer in the British Army. She spent some of her youth in Ireland – her father was posted to Dublin in 1882 – and formed a great attachment to the country and its people. During her time there she witnessed the eviction of a family from their home and was greatly affected by it – throughout her life she worked for the improvement of the conditions of the poor and downtrodden.

On 30 January 1889, Yeats met Maud Gonne for the first time. She arrived at his family home in Blenheim Road in London, bearing an introduction from John O'Leary, intent on telling the young writer how much she admired *The Island of Statues*. The confident, well-travelled young woman was beautiful and flamboyant – tall with red hair and a wonderful complexion, according to contemporary accounts – and had received several marriage proposals before she was 18. She was passionately dedicated to the cause of Irish nationalism, which was close to Yeats's heart, although his nationalism was more philosophical, while hers was active (she campaigned vigorously for Home Rule for Ireland).

For Yeats this encounter was a life-changer, love at first sight, a *coup de foudre*, the beginning of an unrequited passion that lasted almost 30 years. He reflected later that this meeting was when 'the troubling of my life began'.

Maud invited Yeats to dine with her that evening, 30 January. They had dinner together every night until she returned to Paris several days later. At that time she was involved in an affair with French right-wing politician Lucien Millevoye, with whom she would have two children, something that she concealed from Yeats for many years.

Maud and Yeats were close friends and confidants. They shared an interest in theosophy and in 1891 Yeats introduced her to the Golden Dawn. They frequently shared the details of their occult experiences with each other. As far as she was concerned, their relationship was not a romantic one, but a platonic union of intellects and souls. If his poetry from the early 1890s can be taken as an indication, it is clear that Yeats did not seem to have expected his romantic feelings to be returned, although he proposed marriage to her no fewer than three times.

In 1891, he prophesied the final burning out of that passion in 'When You Are Old':

When you are old and grey and full of sleep,
And nodding by the fire, take down this book,
And slowly read, and dream of the soft look
Your eyes had once, and of their shadows deep;

How many loved your moments of glad grace,
And loved your beauty with love false or true,
But one man loved the pilgrim soul in you,
And loved the sorrows of your changing face;

And bending down beside the glowing bars,
Murmur, a little sadly, how Love fled
And paced upon the mountains overhead
And hid his face amid a crowd of stars.

He expresses similar sentiments in 'In Memory of Your Dream One July Night':

My world was fallen and over, for your dark soft
eyes on it shone;
A thousand years it had waited and now it is gone,
it is gone.

Less than a year after meeting Yeats for the first time in London, Maud had a child with Millevoye, a boy called Georges, who died before he was two. She was unable to hide her grief from Yeats and told him what had happened, but said that she had adopted a son who had died.

In 1892, Yeats published his play about Ireland, *Cathleen Ni Houlihan*. He said that Maud was the inspiration for its heroine.

In 1894, she was pregnant by Millevoye again, this time with a daughter, Iseult. Despite their connection, she once again concealed her child's birth from Yeats. She didn't tell him the truth about Millevoye and the two children they had together until 1898, when she and Yeats were in Dublin at the same time. This was when they kissed for the first time – afterwards he proposed, but Maud told him that she could never

Lucien Millevoye in a cartoon from *L'Assiette au Beurre*

marry him. She always told him that she had a horror of the physical act of love. Having heard the story of her affair with Millevoye, it is hard to believe that he would have accepted this as the truth. Maud told friends that although she loved Yeats as a dear friend, she could never contemplate marrying him. She believed that unrequited love had honed his skill as a poet, and said that 'Poets should never marry. The world should thank me for not marrying you.'

Although they solemnised their spiritual union on an astral plane, Yeats seems to have accepted the fact that Maud would never marry him or engage in a romantic relationship with him. He must have been devastated by her revelations – he had erected for her a pedestal of purity and uprightness and defended her, especially in his poetry, to all those who called her reputation into question.

Lucien Millevoye

He Thinks of Those Who
Have Spoken Evil of His Beloved

Half close your eyelids, loosen your hair,
And dream about the great and their pride;
They have spoken against you everywhere,
But weigh this song with the great and their pride;
I made it out of a mouthful of air,
Their children's children shall say they have lied.

Portrait of Lady Lavery as *Kathleen
Ni Houlihan* by John Lavery, 1928

Then, in 1903, despite her stated aversion to sex, Maud married Major John MacBride, who had organised the Irish Transvaal Brigade to fight alongside the Boers against the British in the Second Boer War of 1899–1903. They met in the US while he was on a fund raising tour. Yeats is said to have been devastated by the marriage, not only because Maud was now lost to him irrevocably, but also because he loathed MacBride.

Their son, Seán MacBride, was born that year, but the marriage was not a success. Maud petitioned for divorce in 1904 because of MacBride's alleged drunkenness and adultery. They were living in Paris and the French courts refused to grant her petition because MacBride had established Irish domicile, complicating the legal situation for his wife. All she was granted was a legal separation and custody of her son. She decided not to take him to Ireland for fear of losing custody there, effectively exiling herself until her husband's death.

In 1908 Maud and Yeats finally slept together – their sexual relationship was short and was ended by Maud. In the

Major John MacBride, painted by Mick O'Dea

aftermath of the 1916 Rising MacBride was executed as one of its leaders and Maud was legally free to marry again if she wished. In July of that year Yeats proposed to Maud a final time, probably more as a matter of form because she was finally unencumbered.

She refused him, yet again. Perhaps his passion had waned by then. In a poem written just a few years later he acknowledged that 'the heart grows old'.

A Song

I thought no more was needed
Youth to prolong
Than Dumb-bell and foil
To keep the body young.
O who could have foretold
That the heart grows old?

Though I have many words,
What woman's satisfied,
I am no longer faint
Because at her side?
O who could have foretold
That the heart grows old?

I have not lost desire
But the heart that I had;
I thought 'twould burn my body
Laid on the death-bed,
For who could have foretold
That the heart grows old?

Not daunted by this final refusal, Yeats asked Maud if he could press his suit with her 23-year-old daughter Iseult. He proposed to the young woman in 1916 and again in 1917 and her refusal seems to have propelled him to look elsewhere for a wife.

We would probably know more of the relationship between Yeats and Maud Gonne had she not taken the anti-Treaty side in the Irish Civil War. Her home at St Stephen's Green was raided by soldiers of the Free State government and most of her papers, including all of Yeats's letters to her over a period of 35 years, were burned. Their political differences (Yeats supported the Free State government) divided them, although they remained in contact for the rest of Yeats's life. He wrote an eloquent tribute to her in 1916, 'No Second Troy'.

Maud Gonne visited Yeats at his home in Rathfarnham in the summer of 1938 – it was their last meeting; five months later he was dead.

No Second Troy

Why should I blame her that she filled my days
With misery, or that she would of late
Have taught to ignorant men most violent ways
Or hurled the little streets upon the great,
Had they but courage equal to desire?
What could have made her peaceful with a mind
That nobleness made simple as a fire,
With beauty like a tightened bow, a kind
That is not natural in an age like this,
Being high and solitary and most stern?
Why, what could she have done, being what she is?
Was there another Troy for her to burn?

CHAPTER 7

Love and Marriage

Olivia Shakespear

I have no child, I have nothing but a book

Perhaps because of his long infatuation with Maud Gonne, Yeats did not have the string of relationships that would have been normal for a young man living in bohemian circles in London in the late 19th century. He was 30 before he lost his virginity to Olivia Shakespear, a beautiful, unhappily married novelist he met in 1894 at a dinner party in London. He was attracted to her immediately – not least among her appealing characteristics was an interest in spiritualism, which did not go as deep as Yeats's own, but at least put her on his wavelength. Yeats, ever the impulsive, if rather naïve romantic, suggested they run away together. He had no money, and if she were to leave her husband she would have been almost penniless.

They didn't consummate the affair for a year after their first meeting. Olivia, probably frustrated by his failure to move things forward, had even found him a private apartment so that they could conduct an affair (this apartment was at 18

Olivia Shakespear's passport photograph

Woburn Buildings, near Euston Station, and it would be Yeats's London base until he moved permanently to Ireland in 1922). Their sexual relationship lasted a year, but then Maud Gonne reinserted herself in Yeats's life and he broke off the affair with Olivia in February 1897.

The Lover Mourns for the Loss of Love

Pale brows, still hands and dim hair,
I had a beautiful friend
And dreamed that the old despair
Would end in love in the end:
She looked in my heart one day
And saw your image was there;
She has gone weeping away.

His unrequited feelings for Maud Gonne were inextricably woven into the fabric of his life and seem to have been an enduring impediment to a lasting relationship with an available woman. Perhaps Maud enjoyed the adulation of the physically striking young writer, which would have become all the more flattering as his success and literary stature increased.

However, in 1908 Yeats embarked on a five-year affair with Mabel Dickinson, a charming and intelligent single Anglo-Irish woman in her early 30s, who worked as a physiotherapist (although some people derided her as having been a masseuse). The relationship was affectionate and intellectual and seems to have made Yeats happy until she wrote to him in 1913 to say that she thought she might be pregnant. It was a false alarm, but Yeats was unable to eat or sleep during the days of uncertainty, and a psychic consultation led him to believe that Mabel was trying to deceive him in order to trick him into marriage. A short while later his good friend Lady Gregory advised him to marry in order to prevent another similar episode and soon she was presenting suitable young women for his inspection. He continued to evade marriage but had a few short affairs.

Shortly after the drama with Mabel he addressed a poem to his 'old fathers', apologising for the fact that he had as yet, produced no heirs, laying the blame at the door of his fruitless pursuit of Maud Gonne.

> Pardon that for a barren passion's sake.
> Although I have come close on forty-nine,
> I have no child, I have nothing but a book,
> Nothing but that to prove your blood and mine.

When in London he still saw Olivia Shakespear, although their relationship was by now almost completely platonic. Like Lady Gregory, she urged him to think about getting married, and as 1917 wore on, he became focused on finding a suitable wife – he was, as ever, guided by the occult, and his personal astrological horoscope identified October of that year as the most auspicious time for him to get married. By now, his earnings from his poetry and lectures allowed him to lead a comfortable lifestyle and would have enabled him to support a wife.

His rush to achieve posterity through marriage brought his thoughts once more to Maud Gonne's young daughter, Iseult.

Lady Gregory

Throughout her life he had cast himself in the role of father figure, although he had become attracted to her during her teens. She had proposed to him, jokingly, in 1909, when she was 15.

By 1916 Iseult was a beautiful young woman, and Yeats was proud to be seen around London with her. When Maud turned down his final proposal in July of that year, he asked if he might propose to Iseult. She consented, but Iseult's response was evasive. He persisted for a year, proposing to her for a second time in August 1917. Again, she was evasive, but after a few weeks, she turned him down definitively. He had been entertaining doubts, in any event, on the grounds of the great disparity in their age (he was 52 to her 22): 'The living beauty is for younger men.' However, it was now September, and Yeats was in a hurry to get married before his astrological deadline in October.

It came as a surprise to Yeats's family and friends when he married Georgie Hyde-Lees (always called 'George' by Yeats, who disliked the name Georgie) on 20 October 1917 at a registry office in Paddington in London. He was not a secretive man, but he had, unusually, given no prior notice of this important event to friends and family. His father in New York was concerned because the bride was so young (she was 25, not much older than Iseult Gonne, but Yeats obviously didn't think that she was sufficiently beautiful to be considered a 'living beauty' for 'younger men'), but he was pleased that she had her own income, certainly enough to match the poet's own. From John Butler Yeats's correspondence with his daughters, it is clear that he thought that marriage would be the making of his eldest son. Maud Gonne said, cuttingly, that he had married 'a good woman of 25 – rich of course – who has to look after him; she might either become his slave or run away from him after a certain length of time.'

George was an intelligent, well-travelled and well-educated (her education was far superior to that of Yeats) young woman with bohemian leanings. She spoke fluent French and Italian (Yeats had always struggled with French, which he wished he could master). Lily Yeats wrote to her father that

> She is not good looking, but is comely, her nose too
> big for good looks; her colour ruddy and her hair
> reddish brown; her eyes very good and fine blue,

> with very dark, strongly marked eyebrows. She is
> quiet but not slow, her brain, I would judge, quick
> and trained and sensitive.

She probably didn't conform to Yeats's idea of a classical beauty. Her father had died some years earlier, but her mother took the precaution of asking Lady Gregory if she thought he was marrying her daughter on the rebound from Iseult Gonne. Gregory, who had been counselling Yeats to marry for years, reassured her and the marriage went ahead, unhindered.

George had been introduced to Yeats by Olivia Shakespear in 1910 or 1911. At the end of 1911 she was undertaking small research jobs for him and accompanying him to séances. The very obvious thing that they had in common was their membership of the Golden Dawn. In 1914 he was her sponsor in an initiation ceremony within the organisation – by 1917 she was level-pegging with him in the same middle rank of the society. He was Frater Demon Est Deus Inversus (DEDI), and she was Soror Nemo. His third marriage proposal in the space of 14 months, in September 1917, may have been third

time lucky. George certainly seems to have been delighted at the prospect of becoming the wife of such a gifted and famous man (An Irish newspaper report, headed 'W. B. Yeats Married', described him as 'perhaps the greatest figure in Anglo-Irish literature'). In any event, most of the young men of George's own generation had died in the Great War. Her interest in astrology probably meant that Yeats's rush to get married in order to fulfil his destiny seemed perfectly reasonable to her.

The couple honeymooned in the Ashdown Forest in Sussex, in a house that Yeats had rented over the years. It became clear that George was expected to be a secretary or amanuensis to her poet husband. Four days into the honeymoon, much to Yeats's delight, George started experimenting with 'automatic writing', a psychic phenomenon whereby the writer's hand and pen are guided by the spirit world. In total, they had more than 400 automatic writing sessions, producing almost 4,000 pages of handwritten text. In his introduction to his great philosophical work, *A Vision*, in which he wove all the threads of the writing into a comprehensive text, Yeats said:

On the afternoon of October 24th, 1917, four
days after my marriage, my wife surprised me
by attempting automatic writing. What came in
disjointed sentences, in almost illegible writing, was so
exciting, sometimes so profound, that I persuaded her
to give an hour or two day after day to the unknown
writer, and after some half dozen such hours offered
to spend what remained of life explaining and piecing
together those scattered sentences.

In the course of their experiments, George said that she
had made contact with a Butler ancestor of Yeats, whose dead
son would be reincarnated in their first child, who would be a
boy. The ancestor claimed to be Anne Hyde, who was married
to a Duke of Ormonde. The baby eventually born to George
and Yeats, on 26 February 1919, was a girl – when she was told
that it wasn't the promised boy, George burst into tears. Yeats,
however, told people he had wanted a daughter. They called her
Anne Butler Yeats. Yeats wrote a long poem for her, entitled 'A
Prayer For My Daughter', the following verses of which have
been especially scorned by feminists:

May she be granted beauty and yet not
Beauty to make a stranger's eye distraught,
Or hers before a looking-glass, for such,
Being made Beautiful overmuch,
Consider beauty a sufficient end,
Lose natural kindness and maybe
The heart-revealing intimacy
That chooses right, and never find a friend.

An intellectual hatred is the worst,
So let her think opinions are accursed.
Have I not seen the loveliest woman born
Out of the mouth of Plenty's horn,
Because of her opinionated mind
Barter that horn and every good
By quiet natures understood
For an old bellows full of angry wind.

When Anne was six months old, George decided that it
was time to have another baby. The spirit guide said that the
couple could have one more child, this time a boy, and that
the conception date would be set during a session of automatic

writing. On 22 August 1921, the anticipated son, Michael, was born. The family was complete, and the automatic writing experiment stopped.

'A Prayer For My Son' has a more pragmatic tone, Yeats's high-blown wishes for his daughter having been tempered by the experience of having an infant in the house.

> Bid a strong ghost stand at the head
> That my son Michael may sleep sound,
> Nor cry, nor turn in the bed
> Till his morning meal come round;
> And may departing twilight keep
> All dread afar till morning's back,
> That his mother may not lack
> Her fill of sleep.

CHAPTER 8

The Celtic Revival

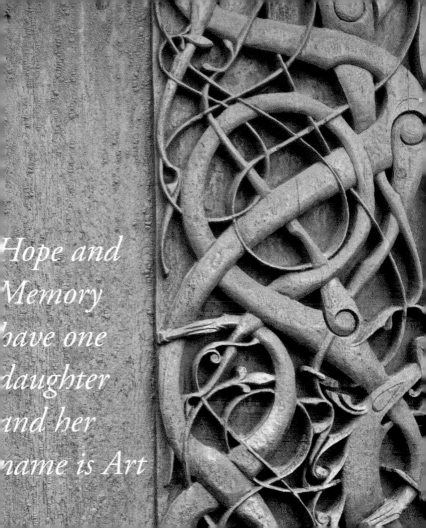

Hope and Memory have one daughter and her name is Art

In 1923, when Yeats was awarded the Nobel Prize for Literature, he told the dignitaries assembled for the prizewinners' banquet:

> Thirty years ago a number of Irish writers met together in societies and began a remorseless criticism of the literature of their country. It was their dream that by freeing it from provincialism they might win for it European recognition.

This is a description of the first stirrings of the Irish Literary Revival, of which Yeats was a leading light. He was seeking to create a cultural renaissance and to bring about a rebirth of Ireland's national identity after the decline of its native language and the subjugation of its people and culture.

From a certain perspective it could be said that 19th-century Ireland is characterised by failure: the failure of the potato crop, which led to the Great Famine; a handful of failed rebellions; and the failure to achieve Home Rule, even though it had been adopted as a policy at Westminster by the

Liberal Party. Ireland's great leader and champion Charles Stewart Parnell died in 1891, creating what Yeats referred to as a 'political vacuum'. As a cultural nationalist he regarded the situation as an opportunity for a flowering of Irish art and literature.

Lady Gregory's bookplate from *Fairy and Folk Tales of the Irish Peasantry*

In 1888 Yeats had published *Fairy and Folk Tales of the Irish Peasantry*, which was a compilation of all the folk tales that had been collected in the 18th and 19th centuries. It was a huge undertaking – Douglas Hyde, an academic folklorist who would become the first president of Ireland in 1938, was Yeats's collaborator in this vast project.

In the beginning, the literary movement had two locations – London and Dublin. In 1892, in London, Yeats founded the Irish Literary Society, with Gavan Duffy and T. W. Rolleston. The same year, in Dublin, he founded the National Literary Society. Douglas Hyde was its first president. As one of the chief organisers, Yeats travelled back and forth between the two cities, writing and organising.

In 1893 Yeats published *The Celtic Twilight*, a collection of folk tales and legends gathered in the west of Ireland where he had spent so much time as a young boy. The final item in the volume was his own poem 'Into the Twilight', a homage to Ireland herself.

Out-worn heart, in a time out-worn,
Come clear of the nets of wrong and right;
Laugh, heart, again in the grey twilight,
Sigh, heart, again in the dew of the morn.

Your mother Eire is always young,
Dew ever shining and twilight grey;
Though hope fall from you and love decay,
Burning in fires of a slanderous tongue.

Come, heart, where hill is heaped upon hill:
For there the mystical brotherhood
Of sun and moon and hollow and wood
And river and stream work out their will;

And God stands winding His lonely horn,
And time and the world are ever in flight;
And love is less kind than the grey twilight,
And hope is less dear than the dew of morn.

This poem and the collection in which it appeared soon gave the Irish Literary Revival its nickname of The Celtic Revival.

It sometimes seems strange to those looking back at the history of the movement that it was, from its inception, organised largely by members of the Protestant, Anglo-Irish ascendancy, which included Yeats. However, this particular segment of society had a very strong sense of the cultural nationalism that defined the revival. It must have been clear that Irish independence could not be deferred by the British government for ever, and the movement was partly about creating a new national identity for the new nation, through the development of a new national literature.

After a while, Dublin began to take the central role in the movement's activities and achievements. This meshed with the wider push towards Irish independence – the people, for so long almost passive pawns of Great Britain, were being encouraged to do for themselves and to think for themselves and to produce a new and vibrant literature for the nation.

Cúchulainn bronze at the GPO, Dublin

The stereotypical image of the Irishman was that of landless peasant, with no ambition and not a great deal of intelligence. Yeats and the revival wanted to reverse the stereotype, tapping into the huge wealth of folk stories and epic tales of mythical heroes. Yeats himself focused on Cúchulain as the great Irish hero, with as much relevance to the modern world as he had to that of the ancients who had conjured him. Cúchulain and the other heroes could instil a new sense of pride in the Irish people. In his introduction to *The Celtic Twilight* Yeats said that he wanted to 'show in a vision something of the face of Ireland to any of my own people who would look where I bid them'.

Ireland's tradition of storytelling up to this point was oral. When Yeats, with Lady Gregory and Edward Martyn, formulated the idea of a national theatre, it was partly to create a new theatrical vehicle for presenting the old tales and to make them relevant to modern times. Many of the early plays produced by the new theatre (which became the Abbey Theatre) provided an introduction to the stories and characters of Irish myth and legend. However, mythology was not the only resource. Far from continuing to put on old plays based on the same ancient tales, the Abbey writers, including Yeats himself, John Millington Synge and Sean O'Casey, formulated new plays on the old themes, bringing them up to date in the context of the times.

From its inception there had been nationalists who derided the literary outpourings of the Abbey writers because they were not writing in the Irish language and were failing to promote a sufficiently hard-line version of nationalism. Yeats's response to this, a defence of artistic independence and integrity, appeared in the *United Irishman* in October 1903.

> Literature is always personal, always one man's vision
> of the world, one man's experience, and it can only be
> popular when men are ready to welcome the vision
> of others. A community that is opinion-ridden, even
> when these opinions are in themselves noble, is likely
> to put its creative minds into some sort of prison.

Synge's *The Playboy of the Western World* provoked outrage from its first airing in 1907, for all the wrong reasons. It is a play that is concerned with the nature of violence and the

Irish tendency to glorify the violent deeds of the past while vilifying those who carry them out in the present. The stirring theme became somewhat lost in the controversy surrounding the author's reference to a female undergarment. The play is remarkable as an example of the move away from the heroes of the past to a questioning of present-day motives. It is an indication, more than anything else, that the revival was a living and developing idea, one that would not be stuck in its glorious past. Yeats, as first president of the theatre, applauded this and supported the Abbey stable of authors in their endeavours to build a truly national theatre.

In his Nobel acceptance speech, Yeats gave a rationale for the literary and dramatic revival that he had spearheaded:

> [W]e thought of everything that was romantic and poetical, because the nationalism we had called up – the nationalism every generation had called up in moments of discouragement – was romantic and poetical.

Harry Clarke's *Geneva Window* depicting *The Playboy of the Western World* by J.M. Synge

A Family Enterprise – The Cuala Press

In the late 19th century, when Lily and Lolly Yeats were still living in London with their parents, they became acquainted with William Morris, one of the founders of the Arts and Crafts movement in Britain. In 1900 they decided to move to Dublin, and in 1902 they joined the Dun Emer arts and the craft cooperative in Dundrum in South County Dublin. Lily was in charge of the embroideries department and Lolly managed the printing press.

Although mechanised printing was fast replacing the old hand-printing techniques, Lolly bought a hand-cranked press and produced everything by hand, following the Arts and Crafts movement's theories of the importance of hand crafting.

In 1908 the sisters decided to part company with Dun Emer to set up their own embroidery workshop and printing press, Cuala, in nearby Churchtown. Once again, Lily managed the embroideries department and Lolly set up the press.

Yeats himself was Cuala's literary editor – it published about 30 of his own works in their first editions. Jack Yeats worked on design and illustration and when Yeats got married, George helped Lily in the embroideries section.

Cuala was staffed entirely by women. It concentrated on producing new works by Irish writers, thus contributing to the success of the Irish Literary Revival. It published over 70 titles, including works by Lady Gregory, J. M. Synge, Katharine Tynan and George Russell. The press also produced booklets, cards, book plates and hand-coloured prints, and an illustrated periodical called *The Broadside*, which published poetry and music. It was not a great financial success and Yeats had to bail it out on several occasions.

George Yeats took over management of the press when Lolly died in 1940 and kept it going until 1946. In 1969 Yeats's two children, Michael and Anne, revived the press and kept it going until the mid-1980s.

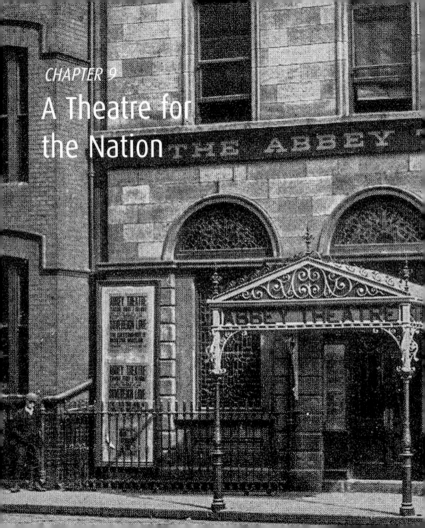

CHAPTER 9

A Theatre for
the Nation

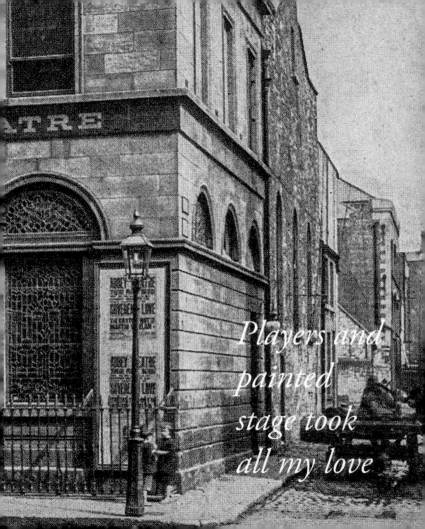

Players and painted stage took all my love

For the first 15 years of the 20th century Yeats was almost completely absorbed in the setting up of a national theatre for Ireland. Although now mainly remembered as a poet, he had always had an interest in drama – his first written works were plays – which was encouraged by his flamboyant and highly dramatic father, and he was an enthusiastic playwright and dramatist throughout his life.

He met Lady Augusta Gregory in 1896 at the home of her neighbour Edward Martyn. In the summer of 1897, he made the first of many visits to her Galway estate, Coole Park. Yeats, his host and Martyn together devised and published the *Manifesto for an Irish Literary Theatre*, which outlined their plans to promote native, innovative Irish poetic drama. At that time the dramatic fare on offer in Ireland provided a bland diet of British comedies of manners and dramas featuring 'stage' Irishmen. Yeats, with his great interest in Irish legends and folklore wanted to provide an alternative by bringing to the Irish stage a renewed cultural

Philanthropist Edward Martyn in a graphite sketch by John Butler Yeats

sense, which would be imbued with his own esoteric philosophies.

In 1898, Yeats, with Lady Gregory, Edward Martyn and George Moore, founded the Irish Literary Theatre in Dublin, with the aim of producing plays by Irish authors. In 1899 they staged the first of three annual productions, including Yeats's *The Countess Cathleen*, in the Antient Concert Rooms at Brunswick Street and the Gaiety Theatre in South King Street.

In 1902 offerings included George Russell's *Deirdre* and Yeats's *Cathleen Ni Houlihan*. These productions met with such success that the producers decided to put things on a formal basis by founding the Irish National Theatre Group in 1903. Yeats was the group's first president, with Lady Gregory and Synge as co-directors.

Annie Horniman

The first performances were put on in the Molesworth Hall in Dublin 2 and were funded by an English benefactor, Annie Horniman, who had been involved in theatrical productions in England. The national theatre was still without a permanent home, but when the Hibernian Theatre of Varieties in Lower Abbey Street became available, Horniman (who was besotted with Yeats) agreed to fund its purchase and a refurbishment that would suit the needs of the society. The Abbey Theatre opened its doors on 27 December 1904, for a week-long run featuring four one-act plays, Yeats's *On Baile's Strand* (one of several treatments of the mythical Irish hero Cúchulain) and *Cathleen Ni Houlihan*, Synge's *In the Shadow of the Glen* and Lady Gregory's *Spreading the News*. The actors are not mentioned on the first playbill advertising the opening plays – Maud Gonne took the title role in *Cathleen Ni Houlihan*. It is recorded that the Dublin audiences took to awarding ratings based on PQ (peasant quality).

As the founding members had hoped, the theatre was used to showcase rising Irish talent, and many of the plays that form the backbone of the repertoire that is now so familiar to Dublin audiences had their first outing on the boards of the Abbey.

Many of the early members of the theatre's board of directors were heavyweights of the literary world, which earned the theatre a reputation as a 'writer's theatre'. Artistic temperaments often led to serious clashes, and Lady Gregory is said to have become adept at pouring oil on troubled waters. Yeats said later, in the course of his Nobel acceptance speech:

> We had little money and at first needed little, twenty-five pounds given by Lady Gregory and twenty pounds by myself and a few pounds picked up here and there. And our theatrical organization was preposterous, players and authors all sat together and settled by vote what play should be performed and who should play it.

Yeats's account of the decision-making process gives an insight into the very pedantic approach that was routinely taken by the organisers.

> Lady Gregory wrote her first comedy. My verse plays were not long enough to fill an evening and so she wrote a little play on a country love story in the dialect of her neighbourhood. A countryman returns from

America with a hundred pounds and discovers his old sweetheart married to a bankrupt farmer. He plays cards with the farmer and, by cheating against himself, gives him the hundred pounds. The company refused to perform that play because they said to admit an emigrant's return with a hundred pounds would encourage emigration. We produced evidence of returned emigrants with much larger sums but were told that only made the matter worse. Then after this interminable argument had worn us all out, Lady Gregory agreed to reduce the sum to twenty and the actors gave way.

Another of Lady Gregory's plays, *The Rising of the Moon*,

> could not be performed for two years because of
> political hostility. A policeman discovers an escaped
> Fenian prisoner and sets him free, because the prisoner
> has aroused with some old songs the half forgotten
> patriotism of his youth. The players would not perform
> it because they said it was an unpatriotic act to admit
> that a policeman was capable of patriotism.

Sometimes the productions had unexpected results. Riots erupted in the theatre on the opening nights of Synge's *Playboy of the Western World* (the play is based on the account of a real event that was related to Synge on a visit to the Aran Islands, off the coast of Galway). Yeats gave an account of the turmoil provoked by the play:

> On Saturday, January 26, 1907, I was lecturing in
> Aberdeen, and when my lecture was over I was given
> a telegram which said, 'Play great success.' It had been
> sent from Dublin after the second act of *The Playboy of
> the Western World*, then being performed for the first

time. After one in the morning, my host brought to my bedroom this second telegram, 'Audience broke up in disorder at the word shift.' I knew no more until I got the Dublin papers on my way from Belfast to Dublin on Tuesday morning. On the Monday night no words of the play had been heard. About forty young men had sat in the front seats of the pit, and stamped and shouted and blown trumpets from the rise to the fall of the curtain. On the Tuesday night also the forty young men were there. They wished to silence what they considered a slander upon Ireland's womanhood.

It was not the last time an Abbey production would provoke riots. In 1926 Sean O'Casey's *The Plough and the Stars* met with such an extreme reaction that the Abbey rejected his next play.

For the first 10 years of the new century Yeats was actively involved in the running of the new theatre company – he selected plays, recruited actors and managers and made arrangements for the company to tour in England and the US. His own output during that time was a staggering 10 plays – one result, derived from the necessity of writing clear and intelligible dialogue for his characters, was the simplification or 'modernisation' of his verse, a move away from the elaborate constructions so loved by the Victorians. He himself said of the new departure in his work that it had got 'more masculine'. His public, who had loved the lyricism of 'He Wishes for the Cloths of Heaven' and 'The Lake Isle of Innisfree' were disappointed with the alteration in style. Yeats, however, was clear that it was a positive thing, writing in 'The Coat', published in 1912,

> I made my song a coat
> Covered with embroideries
> Out of old mythologies
> From heel to throat;
> But the fools caught it,
> Wore it in the world's eyes
> As though they'd wrought it.
> Song, let them take it,
> For there's more enterprise
> In walking naked.

Meanwhile, in 1909, Lennox Robinson had taken over as manager and director of the Abbey. He regarded Yeats as writer with 'an unerring eye for situation', and reminisced that the poet once told him that the only dramatist he really admired was Shakespeare.

In 1910, the theatre's main benefactor, Annie Horniman, withdrew her support when the theatre refused to close as a mark of respect when King Edward VII died. Public interest and box office returns dipped and the Abbey struggled for funding until 1924, when Yeats and Lady Gregory offered it to the Free State government as a gift. It was reluctantly accepted – the decision in favour of doing so was made on the basis of the theatre's commitment to an Irish-language repertoire. The Abbey thus became the first state-maintained theatre in the English-speaking world and it is now funded by the Arts Council of Ireland.

Yeats's commitment to Ireland's national theatre lasted almost to the end of his life – as late as 1935 he was still involved in its ethos and management. In 1938, just a few months before his death, he attended the Abbey for the final time to see the première of his play *Purgatory*.

The theatre went into something of a creative decline after his death, but it recovered its equilibrium after several decades and it continues to maintain the high literary ideals of its founders.

When the theatre first opened its doors in 1904, Yeats commissioned Elinor Mary Monsell to create a woodcut engraving using images from Irish mythology. The result depicts the Irish Wolfhound (the symbol of Ireland) with Queen Maeve – in the right-hand corner there is a rising sun. Adopted as the Abbey's logo, it still represents the national theatre today.

CHAPTER 10

A Lasting Friendship – Lady Gregory

snow in the autumn leaves
Coole Park, County Galway

She has been
to me mother,
friend, sister
and brother

One of the most important relationships in Yeats's life was his friendship with Lady Augusta Gregory, which lasted 36 years, from their first meeting in 1896 until her death in 1932. Yeats was 31 and Lady Gregory was 45. She became his friend and confidante, encouraged and directed him in his literary endeavours and collaborated with him on major cultural projects. She is now remembered for that friendship and as one of the driving forces behind the national literary revival of the late 19th and early 20th centuries. She was also, with Yeats, a founder of Ireland's national theatre.

Although, like Yeats, Lady Gregory belonged to the Anglo-Irish ascendancy, her background was very different from his. Born Isabella Augusta Persse to a family of landowners with an estate at Roxborough, County Galway, she had an Irish-speaking nanny who was probably the reason for her lifelong interest in Irish history, language and folklore. She married a widower, Sir William Gregory, in 1880. He shared her interest in the arts and in literature, and they hosted a renowned literary salon in London.

After their marriage the Gregorys travelled widely together and Lady Gregory began to write short stories and poems. When Sir William died in 1892, she returned to his estate at Coole Park to edit his memoirs. In 1893 she visited the Aran Islands off the Galway coast and her interest in Irish folklore and language resurfaced. An unlikely republican nationalist, the work she carried out on the correspondence of her husband's family gave her an insight into the history of her country that provoked in her a 'dislike and distrust of England'.

Lady Gregory met Yeats at Tullyra Castle, County Galway, while he was visiting her neighbour, Edward Martyn, a playwright and ardent nationalist. The young poet described her as 'a plainly dressed woman of forty-five, without obvious good looks, except the charm that comes from strength, intelligence and kindness'. She had read and been impressed by Yeats's work, particularly *The Celtic Twilight*, and invited him to Coole Park – that invitation was the first of many and Yeats enjoyed her hospitality during many extended stays there. His first visit coincided with a bout of ill health, so instead of working, he accompanied his hostess on her rounds of local cottages, collecting folk tales and legends – a later edition of *The Celtic Twilight* would incorporate much of the lore gleaned on this trip.

The beautiful Coole estate was, naturally, the backdrop to, and inspiration for many of his poems. Nineteen years after his first visit, Yeats looked back on some of the time he had spent there.

The Wild Swans at Coole

The trees are in their autumn beauty,
The woodland paths are dry,
Under the October twilight the water
Mirrors a still sky;
Upon the brimming water among the stones
Are nine-and-fifty swans.

The nineteenth autumn has come upon me
Since I first made my count;
I saw, before I had well finished,
All suddenly mount
And scatter wheeling in great broken rings
Upon their clamorous wings.

I have looked upon those brilliant creatures,
And now my heart is sore.
All's changed since I, hearing at twilight,
The first time on this shore,

The bell-beat of their wings above my head,
Trod with a lighter tread.

Unwearied still, lover by lover,
They paddle in the cold
Companionable streams or climb the air;
Their hearts have not grown old;
Passion or conquest, wander where they will,
Attend upon them still.

But now they drift on the still water,
Mysterious, beautiful;
Among what rushes will they build,
By what lake's edge or pool
Delight men's eyes when I awake some day
To find they have flown away.

Yeats and Lady Gregory shared a strong commitment to the idea of a national literary revival and much of their enthusiasm was channelled into the setting up of a national theatre.

But their friendship was far more than an intellectual one. Yeats confided in her about his love affairs and she was in the habit of giving him sound, practical advice, although this was rarely acted upon. As he wrote to her in detail about any developments in his relationship with Maud Gonne, she must have concluded that he was being kept on a string by someone who was not interested in him but was unwilling to lose his adulation. However, quite apart from advice, his friend provided him with a base at Coole Park. The peace and solitude he found there inspired his writing and, for a period of some years, the 17th-century house became his permanent summer home.

Unrequited love shook the foundations of Yeats's mental health, which also affected his physical health. At a difficult time in his life, when his inner turmoil might have overwhelmed his creative impulse, Lady Gregory provided a well-run home whenever he needed it, with a proper routine and a wholesome diet. Whenever he went back to London she sent him food parcels. She lent him money when he needed it, although he was reluctant to take it, not being in a position to repay her. She was, without a doubt, a stabilising influence, and much of Yeats's output during the period of their friendship before his marriage in 1917 is probably at least partly attributable to her care and support.

When Lady Gregory's only son, Robert Gregory, an airman, was killed in Italy in 1918, a casualty of the First World War, Yeats wrote a poignant poem in his memory, one of four of which Gregory's son is the subject.

An Irish Airman Foresees His Death

I know that I shall meet my fate
Somewhere among the clouds above;
Those that I fight I do not hate,
Those that I guard I do not love;
My country is Kiltartan Cross,
My countrymen Kiltartan's poor,
No like end could bring them loss
Or leave them happier than before.
Nor law, nor duty bade me fight,
Nor public men, nor cheering crowds,
A lonely impulse of delight
Drove to this tumult in the clouds;
I balanced all, brought all to mind,
The years to come seem waste of breath,
A waste of breath the years behind
In balance with this life, this death.

In 1909 it had seemed that Lady Gregory's practical and intellectual support would come to an end. Robert wrote to Yeats to tell him that his mother was ill and was not expected to live. The prospect of her death was devastating to her friend, who wrote in his journal:

> I thought my mother was ill and that my sister was asking me to come at once: then I remembered that my mother died years ago and that more than kin was at stake. She has been to me mother, friend, sister and brother. I cannot realize the world without her.

On this occasion Lady Gregory recovered, but in 1931 she was diagnosed with a return of the breast cancer that had first appeared several years earlier. Yeats went to Coole Park and stayed there until her death in May 1932, despite the inconvenience to his family. He was devastated when she died. At her request, he had written a poem about Coole Park, which is his lasting epitaph to his great friend.

Lady Gregory portrait by William Orpen. c1904

Coole Park, 1929

I meditate upon a swallow's flight,
Upon an aged woman and her house,
A sycamore and lime-tree lost in night
Although the western cloud is luminous,
Great works constructed there in nature's spite
For scholars and for poets after us,
Thoughts long knitted into a single thought,
A dance-like glory that those walls begot.

There Hyde before he had beaten into prose
That noble blade the Muses buckle on,
There one that ruffled in his manly pose
For all his timid heart, there that slow man,
That meditative man, John Synge, and those
Impetuous men, Shawe-Taylor and Hugh Lane,
Found pride established in humility,
A scene well set and excellent company.

They came like swallows and like swallows went,
And yet a powerful woman's character
Could keep a swallow to its first intent;
And half a dozen in formation there,
That seemed to swirl upon a compass-point,
Found certainty upon the dreaming air,
The intellectual sweetness of those lines
That cut through time or cross it withershins.

Here, traveller, scholar, poet, take your stand
When all those rooms and passages are gone,
When nettles wave upon a shapeless mound
And saplings root among the broken stone,
And delicate – eyes bent upon the ground,
Back turned upon the brightness of the sun
And all the sensuality of the shade –
A moment's memory to that laurelled head.

Yeats made no more visits to Coole Park.
The house had been sold to the Forestry
Commission before Lady Gregory's death
and she had been living there as a tenant.
The place where so much of the work of the
Irish Literary Revival had taken form was
demolished in the 1940s, although the estate
is now maintained as a nature reserve.

CHAPTER 11

The Land of Heart's Desire

Come take me out
of this dull world

Yeats's association with the county of Sligo in the west of Ireland is so strong that the region is known as 'Yeats country'. His mother's family, the Pollexfens, lived there, and his parents were married in the Church of Ireland cathedral in Sligo town. Yeats spent a large part of his childhood at his mother's family home, which looked out towards the unique outline of the magnificent Ben Bulben. His mother loved Sligo more than any other place and her eldest son seems to have inherited her affection for this part of Ireland. He spent many hours wandering the countryside, deep in thought, and he would later refer to Sligo as 'the Land of Heart's Desire', after his early play of that title, first performed in London in 1894. Some of the lines convey a strong impression of the sense of freedom he must have experienced on his solitary wanderings.

> Faeries, come take me out of this dull world,
> For I would ride with you upon the wind,
> Run on the top of the dishevelled tide,
> And dance upon the mountains like a flame.

As a young adult Yeats was fortunate enough to be able to revisit Sligo frequently, staying in Lissadell House, the childhood home of the revolutionary and Member of Parliament Constance Gore-Booth, later Countess Markiewicz, overlooking Drumcliff Bay. When he was a child he had visited Lissadell whenever his family was installed with his Pollexfen grandparents in Sligo – he and his brother Jack went to the Gore-Booth estate to play cricket. There was also a connection on the Yeats side – his great-grandfather, John Butler Yeats, was rector of nearby Drumcliff when Lissadell House was built in the 1830s. Yeats remembered his childhood visits to 'a very pleasant, kindly, inflammable family, ever ready to take up new ideas and new things'.

Looking back on the time he spent at Lissadell, he immortalised the house and two of the five Gore-Booth siblings, Constance and her suffragette sister Eva, in the poem 'In Memory of Eva Gore-Booth and Con Markiewicz':

The light of evening, Lissadell,
Great windows open to the south,
Two girls in silk kimonos, both
Beautiful, one a gazelle.
But a raving autumn shears
Blossom from the summer's wreath;
The older is condemned to death,
Pardoned, drags out lonely years
Conspiring among the ignorant.
I know not what the younger dreams –
Some vague Utopia – and she seems,
When withered old and skeleton-gaunt,
An image of such politics.
Many a time I think to seek
One or the other out and speak
Of that old Georgian mansion, mix
Pictures of the mind, recall

That table and the talk of youth,
Two girls in silk kimonos, both
Beautiful, one a gazelle.

Dear shadows, now you know it all,
All the folly of a fight
With a common wrong or right.
The innocent and the beautiful
Have no enemy but time;
Arise and bid me strike a match
And strike another till time catch;
Should the conflagration climb,
Run till all the sages know.
We the great gazebo built,
They convicted us of guilt;
Bid me strike a match and blow.

The countryside of Sligo was the landscape that surrounded Yeats as he grew up and it features heavily in his earlier poetry. It inspired 'The Lake Isle of Inisfree', and nearby Hazelwood Demesne is the setting for 'The Song of Wandering Aengus'.

I went out to the hazel wood,
Because a fire was in my head,
And cut and peeled a hazel wand
And hooked a berry to a thread;
And when the moths were on the wing,
And moth-like stars were flickering out,
I dropped the berry in a stream
And caught a little silver trout.

When I had laid it on the floor
I went to blow the fire aflame,
But something rustled on the floor,
And some one called me by my name:
It had become a glimmering girl
With apple blossom in her hair
Who called me by my name and ran
And faded through the brightening air.

Though I am old with wandering
Through hollow lands and hilly lands,
I will find out where she has gone,
And kiss her lips and take her hands;
And walk among the long dappled grass,
And pluck till time and times are done
The silver apples of the sun,
The golden apples of the moon.

Dooney Rock Forest Park is now a pleasant nature reserve but it is also famous as the inspiration for Yeats's light-hearted and rhythmic poem 'The Fiddler of Dooney':

When I play on my fiddle in Dooney,
Folk dance like the wave of the sea;
My cousin is priest in Kilvarnet,
My brother in Mocharabuiee.

I passed my brother and cousin:
They read in their books of prayer;
I read in my book of songs
I bought at the Sligo fair.

When we come to the end of time
To Peter sitting in state,
He will smile on the three old spirits,
But call me first through the gate;

For the good are always the merry,
Save by an evil chance,
And the merry love the fiddle,
And the merry love to dance;

And when the folk there spy me,
They will all come up to me,
With 'Here is the Fiddler of Dooney!'
And dance like a wave of the sea.

Glencar Waterfall features in 'The Stolen Child' as the place

where the wandering water gushes
From the hills above Glen-Car
In pools among the rushes
That scarce could bathe a star

Glencar Waterfall

Although Yeats spent a lot of time in Sligo during his childhood and young adulthood, he rarely went there as he got older, making just one short visit with his wife soon after their marriage. However, he expressed a wish to be buried there, and just under 10 years after his death he was interred in the cemetery attached to his great-grandfather's church at Drumcliff, under the shadow of the great Ben Bulben. A year before his death he wrote 'Under Ben Bulben', the first two lines of which contain specific instructions for his resting place:

> Under bare Ben Bulben's head
> In Drumcliff churchyard Yeats is laid.

CHAPTER 12

An Ideal Poor Man's House – Thoor Ballylee

*To go
elsewhere
is to leave
beauty
behind*

At Ballylee, just few miles to the north of Lady Gregory's estate at Coole Park stands a 14th-century Anglo-Norman stone keep, a square tower with four floors and two small adjoining cottages. Yeats first had the idea of buying it in 1915, but he assured Lady Gregory that he would go ahead with the purchase only if he were thinking of getting married. Perhaps he anticipated that it would be a wedding gift for his future (as yet unidentified) wife. He loved the isolated setting of the tower, but did not relish the idea of living there on his own.

However, in 1917, with the need to marry pressing upon him, he bought Ballylee Castle for £35. By this time Yeats had a respectable annual income of about £500, and even though he was repaying his debts and providing occasional financial support to his impecunious father in New York, he was no longer a struggling poet. Although still maintaining a place in London, he thought that the two cottages would provide holiday accommodation for family and friends, while the tower itself would be ideal as a writer's studio.

Yeats renamed his purchase Túr Ballylee, which was anglicised to Thoor Ballylee. It was always referred to by Yeats, his family and friends as, simply, 'the Tower'. The tower was very dilapidated – the restoration work, starting with the roof, took two years and cost more than anticipated. In September 1918, Yeats and George moved into Ballylee and he wrote a poem to mark the occasion – it incorporated a curse on anyone who might in the future spoil the view.

Grounds at Thoor Ballylee through a window

A Prayer on Going into My House

God grant a blessing on this tower and cottage
And on my heirs, if all remain unspoiled,
No table or chair or stool not simple enough
For shepherd lads in Galilee; and grant
That I myself for portions of the year
May handle nothing and set eyes on nothing
But what the great and passionate have used
Throughout so many varying centuries
We take it for the norm; yet should I dream
Sinbad the sailor's brought a painted chest,
Or image, from beyond the Loadstone Mountain,
That dream is a norm; and should some limb of the Devil
Destroy the view by cutting down an ash
That shades the road, or setting up a cottage
Planned in a government office, shorten his life,
Manacle his soul upon the Red Sea bottom.

Ballylee was never intended to be a permanent home, just a summer house, and living conditions were primitive when the family first moved in – there was no plumbing or running water, and no well, so all the washing water needed by the household had to be fetched from the river and all the drinking water from a source. The toilet was an earth closet and there was no electricity. In the cool Irish summer the moisture seeped through the walls and it must have been an unhealthy environment for a baby. Peat fires and oil stoves just about kept the dampness at bay. The shops, for even the most basic groceries, were several miles away.

However, despite the inconvenience and discomfort, Ballylee had two great advantages – it was close to Coole Park and Lady Gregory, and it was in a beautiful place. Yeats wrote that 'with the hawthorn in blossom all along the river banks, everything is so beautiful that to go elsewhere is to leave beauty behind'.

Yeats was meticulous in his approach to the restoration of the tower. He was greatly influenced by William Morris and the Arts and Crafts movement – the rooms are simply whitewashed and the sparse furniture was plain and handcrafted locally. He wrote to Maud Gonne that

> I dream of making a house that may encourage people to avoid ugly manufactured things – an ideal poor man's house. Except a very few things imported as models we should get all made in Galway or Limerick.

Yeats wrote a poem that was intended to be and in fact was carved on a stone on one of the exterior walls of the tower.

To Be Carved On a Stone
at Thoor Ballylee

I, the poet William Yeats,
With old mill boards and sea-green slates,
And smithy work from the Gort forge,
Restored this tower for my wife George.
And may these characters remain
When all is ruin once again.

Yeats and George spent long periods at Ballylee with their children, Anne and Michael. His love for the place is evident in the wonderful poetry he wrote there, and a mirror-image illustration of the tower appears on the Cuala Press edition of the collection of poems aptly entitled *The Tower*. Acknowledging the significance of the work Yeats did there, another Irish Nobel laureate, Seamus Heaney, said that Thoor Ballylee was the most important building in Ireland.

Coole Park and Ballylee, 1931

Under my window-ledge the waters race,
Otters below and moor-hens on the top,
Run for a mile undimmed in Heaven's face
Then darkening through 'dark' Raftery's 'cellar' drop,
Run underground, rise in a rocky place
In Coole demesne, and there to finish up
Spread to a lake and drop into a hole.
What's water but the generated soul?

Upon the border of that lake's a wood
Now all dry sticks under a wintry sun,
And in a copse of beeches there I stood,
For Nature's pulled her tragic buskin on
And all the rant's a mirror of my mood:
At sudden thunder of the mounting swan
I turned about and looked where branches break
The glittering reaches of the flooded lake.

Another emblem there! That stormy white
But seems a concentration of the sky;
And, like the soul, it sails into the sight
And in the morning's gone, no man knows why;
And is so lovely that it sets to right
What knowledge or its lack had set awry,
So arrogantly pure, a child might think
It can be murdered with a spot of ink.

Sound of a stick upon the floor, a sound
From somebody that toils from chair to chair;
Beloved books that famous hands have bound,
Old marble heads, old pictures everywhere;
Great rooms where travelled men and children found
Content or joy; a last inheritor
Where none has reigned that lacked a name and fame
Or out of folly into folly came.

A spot whereon the founders lived and died
Seemed once more dear than life; ancestral trees,
Or gardens rich in memory glorified
Marriages, alliances and families,
And every bride's ambition satisfied.
Where fashion or mere fantasy decrees
We shift about – all that great glory spent –
Like some poor Arab tribesman and his tent.

We were the last romantics – chose for theme
Traditional sanctity and loveliness;
Whatever's written in what poet's name
The book of the people; whatever most can bless
The mind of man or elevate a rhyme;
But all is changed, that high horse riderless,
Though mounted in that saddle Homer rode
Where the swan drifts upon a darkening flood.

After Yeats's death Thoor Ballylee was neglected and fell 'into ruin once again', although it was purchased by the Kiltartan Society in the 1960s and was restored in time for the celebration of the centenary of Yeats's birth in 1965. His son, Michael, who had spent many a happy childhood summer there, officially opened the restored tower.

CHAPTER 13

Romantic Ireland –
Yeats and Nationalism

Portrait of John O'Leary (1830–1907),
by John Butler Yeats

*A terrible
beauty is born*

In 1885 Yeats met John O'Leary, an Irish patriot who had rebelled against the British government in 1848 and was deputy leader of the Irish Republican Brotherhood (IRB) for three years. In 1866 he was convicted of treason and sentenced to 20 years' imprisonment. The sentence was commuted to exile from Ireland in 1870, and O'Leary lived in Paris until 1885.

Set to resume his fight for his country's liberation when he returned to Ireland, he found that the movement had been undermined by Charles Stewart Parnell's efforts to secure the promise of Home Rule for Ireland, which would establish an Irish parliament with authority to decide on Irish affairs. This meant that there was no longer any point in the nationalist rebellion that O'Leary had once advocated. He turned his energies to other pursuits, encouraging the young writers of the day with his enthusiasm for Irish literature, music and songs. This was the beginning of what might be called Yeats's 'cultural'

ationalism. For the young poet, John O'Leary represented
ll that was good about 'romantic Ireland', and he submerged
imself in the old myths and tales of heroes, recycling them
yrically in his poetry.

Yeats, like his family, was a supporter of Home Rule,
elieving that it would allow the Irish to develop their sense
f nationhood, even though old nationalists like O'Leary felt
hat it didn't go far enough, and would set Catholics against
'rotestants, creating a North-South divide. Yeats believed that
-Iome Rule would, on the contrary, undermine the tradition
hat had pit one group against the other for centuries.

harles Stewart Parnell
ddressing the Irish
'arliament

Yeats left Dublin in 1887, moving to London with his family. He met Maud Gonne there in 1889 and was infected to some degree with her active brand of nationalism, but he was never an ardent supporter of armed rebellion. The nationalism he espoused was more to do with the cultural heritage of the nation than any political expression of nationhood. He further distanced himself from the cause of Irish republicanism when Maud Gonne, much to his dismay, married the soldier and nationalist John MacBride in 1903.

In the early years of the 20th century, while rebellion was being planned under the radar, Yeats was concentrating his efforts on the Irish Literary Revival and the setting up of a national theatre. He, like so many Irish people, was taken completely by surprise when an uprising took place on Easter Monday 1916. Most of the population was bemused and angry at the destruction and believed, with the British government, that it was a despicable act in time of war (the First World War was still raging in Europe, and many Irishmen were fighting on the British side). Yeats thought that the rebellion was brave but foolish.

When the 16 leaders of the uprising (including John MacBride) were executed, the public attitude changed. Yeats's poem 'Sixteen Dead Men' caught the prevailing mood.

> O but we talked at large before
> The sixteen men were shot,
> But who can talk of give and take,
> What should be and what not
> While those dead men are loitering there
> To stir the boiling pot?

The Rising seems to have roused him from a complacency about nationalism and republicanism. One of his most famous poems, 'Easter 1916', published in 1920, endorsed the courageous idealism of the revolutionaries and enhanced Yeats's republican credentials, firmly establishing him in the mind of the Irish public as the 'poet of the revolution'.

> I have met them at close of day
> Coming with vivid faces
> From counter or desk among grey
> Eighteenth-century houses.

I have passed with a nod of the head
Or polite meaningless words,
Or have lingered awhile and said
Polite meaningless words.
And thought before I had done
Of a mocking tale or a gibe
To please a companion
Around the fire at the club,
Being certain that they and I
But lived where motley is worn:
All changed, changed utterly:
A terrible beauty is born.

That woman's days were spent
In ignorant good-will,
Her nights in argument
Until her voice grew shrill.
What voice more sweet than hers
When, young and beautiful,
She rode to harriers?
This man had kept a school
And rode our wingèd horse;

This other his helper and friend
Was coming into his force;
He might have won fame in the end,
So sensitive his nature seemed,
So daring and sweet his thought.
This other man I had dreamed
A drunken vainglorious lout.
He had done most bitter wrong
To some who are near my heart,
Yet I number him in the song;
He, too, has resigned his part
In the casual comedy;
He, too, has been changed in his turn,
Transformed utterly:
A terrible beauty is born.

Hearts with one purpose alone
Through summer and winter seem
Enchanted to a stone
To trouble the living stream.
The horse that comes from the road,
The rider, the birds that range

From cloud to tumbling cloud,
Minute by minute they change;
A shadow of cloud on the stream
Changes minute by minute;
A horse-hoof slides on the brim,
And a horse plashes within it;
The long-legged moor-hens dive,
And hens to moor-cocks call;
Minute by minute they live:
The stone's in the midst of all.

Too long a sacrifice
Can make a stone of the heart.
O when may it suffice?
That is Heaven's part, our part
To murmur name upon name,
As a mother names her child
When sleep at last has come
On limbs that had run wild.
What is it but nightfall?
No, no, not night but death;
Was it needless death after all?

For England may keep faith
For all that is done and said.
We know their dream; enough
To know they dreamed and are dead;
And what if excess of love
Bewildered them till they died?
I write it out in a verse –
MacDonagh and MacBride
And Connolly and Pearse
Now and in time to be,
Wherever green is worn,
Are changed, changed utterly:
A terrible beauty is born.

Padraig Pearse

Yeats maintained a low profile politically during the War of Independence that followed the 1916 Rising, and he didn't publish 'Easter 1916' until 1921, although he read it to gatherings of his friends. When the Irish Free State was established under the Anglo-Irish Treaty of 1922, Yeats was an enthusiastic supporter, although it partitioned the island of Ireland, and his stance caused a lasting rift with his brother Jack, who took the anti-Treaty side. Yeats, because of his youthful involvement with the Young Ireland Society and the Irish Republican Brotherhood, was appointed to Seanad Éireann, the upper house of the new Free State government, and he accepted the nomination, even though a violent civil war had erupted between pro- and anti-Treaty factions and government figures were at risk of being kidnapped and murdered.

A Black and Tan on duty in Dublin, posing with a Lewis gu

His appointment to the Senate brought Yeats permanently back to Ireland from London, where he had kept a home for 30 years. Armed government guards were placed outside his door to protect him from attack or abduction. He was a senator of the Irish Free State for six years. He gives us a glimpse of his government persona in 'Among School Children', written after an official visit to a school and published in 1928.

> I walk through the long schoolroom questioning;
> A kind old nun in a white hood replies;
> The children learn to cipher and to sing,
> To study reading-books and histories,
> To cut and sew, be neat in everything
> In the best modern way – the children's eyes
> In momentary wonder stare upon
> A sixty-year-old smiling public man.

CHAPTER 14

Senator Yeats

I feel I have become a personage

The Anglo-Irish Treaty was signed in London in December 1921, establishing the Irish Free State with dominion status. The country immediately split into two factions, for and against the Treaty. During the nervous months that preceded the outbreak of a bloody civil war Yeats brought his family to Thoor Ballylee, where they lived quietly, George gardening, Yeats writing. Both sides came knocking on the door of the tower house on different occasions. Yeats, a supporter of the Treaty side, was convincingly neutral in his response and they went away. He wrote of the experience in the fifth section of 'Meditations in Time of Civil War'.

The Road at My Door

An affable Irregular
A heavily-built Falstaffian man,
Comes cracking jokes of civil war
As though to die by gunshot were
The finest play under the sun.

A brown Lieutenant and his men,
Half dressed in national uniform,
Stand at my door, and I complain
Of the foul weather, hail and rain,
A pear-tree broken by the storm.

I count those feathered balls of soot
The moor-hen guides upon the stream,
To silence the envy in my thought;
And turn towards my chamber, caught
In the cold snows of a dream.

One night Republicans blew up the old bridge beside the house, bidding the Yeats family a polite good night as they departed the scene of destruction. The rubble from the explosion dammed the river and the ground floor of the house was flooded. The family departed for their new house at 82 Merrion Square.

In 1922, Yeats, a one-time member of the IRB and a supporter of the Irish Free State, was appointed to Seanad Éireann, on the recommendation of his friend Oliver St John Gogarty, also a senator. Yeats, who had just been awarded honorary degrees by Queen's University, Belfast and Trinity College Dublin, was delighted to have been honoured in this way, writing to Olivia Shakespear that 'I feel I have become a personage' (he was not short of honours – in 1915 he turned down a knighthood). The annual stipend of £350 was also welcome to the almost perennially cash-strapped poet.

The upper house of the Irish legislature was provided for in the new Irish Free State constitution. Yeats was one of about 60 Protestants appointed to the Seanad, which, as the second house of the Free State parliament, could debate any proposed legislation introduced by the Dáil but had no veto.

When Yeats was appointed, holding public office was fraught with danger. Despite the armed government guards stationed outside his front door in Merrion Square, shots were fired through a window of the house on one occasion. Government officials and their families ran a huge risk of being kidnapped, burned out of their homes, or even murdered. Yeats wrote to a friend:

> At the Senate house I have for near neighbours two senators, one of whom has had his house bombed for being a senator, and one is under sentence of death because he owns the *Freeman's Journal*.

Maud Gonne, a Republican, was arrested and imprisoned. She wrote to Yeats that she would have nothing more to do with him if he refused to denounce the government. The Yeats family mirrored families all over the country at the time, as brother pitted himself against brother. Jack Yeats, now living in Greystones, County Wicklow, supported the anti-Treaty side,

Maud Gonne McBride on Red Cross duty during the Irish Civil War

and although relations between the brothers remained civil, they were not close.

Yeats was an enthusiastic senator during the six years between his appointment and his retirement in 1928. He attended many of the Seanad sessions, but wrote to a friend that

> I shall speak very little but probably intrigue a great deal to get some old projects into action.

He confined his projects to areas in which he had both an interest and a measure of expertise and he served on many committees: those for the preservation of Irish manuscripts and historic Irish buildings and those that looked after the interests of the National Gallery of Art and the National Museum. He also worked on the copyright committee, and between 1926 and 1928 he chaired the committee responsible for new coinage for the new state – the beautiful coins, designed by Percy Metcalfe after an open competition, were minted in London. They had the Free State symbol of the harp and 'Saorstát Éireann' on one side, while the British monarch's head on the reverse of the coins was replaced by images from the Irish bestiary. The beautiful designs were a long-lasting gift to the nation, with some being carried over to the decimal coinage when it was introduced in 1971 (Yeats himself appeared, alongside the Abbey Theatre logo, on the £20 note released on that occasion). They became redundant when Ireland joined the Eurozone in 2001.

Yeats prepared his Seanad speeches carefully and rehearsed them meticulously at home in front of George. An eye witness remembered his 'mellifluous and slightly ironic tone' whenever he was speaking. His most impassioned speech from the floor of the Seanad was in 1925 on the subject of the introduction of a divorce ban. When the Free State government was formed, divorce was, in theory, available throughout the state, but in 1925 the government, happy to toe the Catholic line, introduced legislation banning divorce, despite the fact that this would deny Protestant citizens, who regarded the issue as a matter for individual conscience, recourse to divorce as a legal remedy. It also ignored the fact that when the Free State constitution had been drawn up those drafting it had refused to enshrine in it the indissolubility of marriage.

Yeats standing at the back with a group of Tailteann Games Visitors at the Royal Irish Academy, 1924

Speaking from a Protestant perspective and always sensitive to the possibility of division between Catholics and Protestants, Yeats delivered an excoriating attack on the government, pointing out that a ban on divorce was a sectarian act that would alienate Northern Irish Protestants.

> It is perhaps the deepest political passion with this nation that North and South be united into one nation. If it ever comes ... the North will not give up any liberty which she already possesses under her constitution ... If you show that this country, Southern Ireland, is going to be governed by Catholic ideas and by Catholic ideas alone, you will never get the North ... You will put a wedge into the midst of this nation ... You will not get the North if you impose on the minority what the minority consider to be oppressive legislation.

> Some of you may probably know that when the committee was set up to draw up the constitution of the Free State, it was urged to incorporate in the constitution the indissolubility of marriage and it refused to do so. That was the expression of the

political mind of Ireland. You are now urged to act
on the advice of men who do not express the political
mind, but who express the religious mind … You are
to force your theology upon persons who are not of
your religion.

I think it is tragic that within three years of this
country gaining its independence we should be
discussing a measure which a minority of this nation
considers to be grossly oppressive.

The bill was passed, and divorce became unavailable in the
Irish Free State and its successor, the Republic of Ireland. The
1937 constitution dedicated the country to the Holy Trinity and
recognised that Roman Catholicism was the religion of the great
majority of the people. Article 41 of that constitution stipulated
that 'no law shall be enacted providing for a grant of dissolution
of marriage'. This remained the case until 1996, when divorce
legislation was introduced following a referendum to amend
the constitution.

CHAPTER 15

Eminence and Illness

Siegfried Loraine Sassoon and W.B. Yeats,
photographed by Lady Ottoline Morrell, 1920

Things fall apart

The 1920s brought great recognition to Yeats, but they also saw the beginning of the health issues that would bother him for the rest of his life. In January 1920 he and George sailed to the US for a lecture tour that also included Canada. His father met George and Yeats saw the old man for the last time (John B. Yeats died in February 1922). The tour was financially rewarding, a help at a time when Yeats was increasingly called upon to provide financial assistance to his ageing father.

On 22 August 1921, George gave birth to Michael Butler Yeats, Yeats's hoped-for son and heir. Despite grave health problems, the infant survived.

After the Anglo-Irish Treaty was signed in December of that year, Yeats was fearful that Ireland would descend into chaos, but was tired of living in Britain and was prepared to move to Dublin, the political situation notwithstanding. 'The Second Coming', written in 1921, gives an insight into his sense of 'things falling apart' in the country of his birth.

Turning and turning in the widening gyre
The falcon cannot hear the falconer
Things fall apart; the centre cannot hold;
Mere anarchy is loosed upon the world,
The blood-dimmed tide is loosed, and everywhere
The ceremony of innocence is drowned.
The best lack all conviction, while the worst
Are full of passionate intensity

In Dublin, George had bought 82 Merrion Square, a spacious townhouse with a prestigious address that gave Yeats the sense of grandeur to which he aspired (he liked to say that the Duke of Wellington was born in Merrion Square, although no facts support this assertion).

The family decamped to the partially renovated Thoor Ballylee in March, returning to Merrion Square in the autumn. November saw the publication of two important collections of Yeats's work, *Later Poems* and *Plays and Prose in Verse*.

In 1922, Yeats became a senator of the Irish Free State when he accepted an appointment to the upper house of the new government. In late 1923 he received the news that he had been awarded the Nobel Prize for literature. In his autobiographies he recounts how the announcement came:

> Early in November (1923) a journalist called to show me a printed paragraph saying that the Nobel Prize would probably be conferred upon Herr Mann, the distinguished novelist, or upon myself. I did not know that the Swedish Academy had ever heard my name.
>
> Then some eight days later between ten and eleven at night, comes the telephone message from the *Irish Times* saying that the prize had indeed been conferred upon me; some ten minutes after that comes a telegram from the Swedish Ambassador; then journalists come for interviews. At half past twelve my wife and I are alone, and search the cellar for a bottle of wine, but it is empty, and as a celebration is necessary we cook sausages.

The editor of *The Irish Times*, who had conveyed the news, recalled that Yeats's first question on being told of the award was

'How much?' (It was a substantial amount – £7,500 – and enabled Yeats to pay off his outstanding debts and invest in some shares.)

The prize was awarded to Yeats for 'his always inspired poetry, which in a highly artistic form gives expression to the spirit of a whole nation'. When the award was presented on 10 December 1923 the president of the Swedish Academy of Sciences addressed the poet:

> What more, then, can I do on this occasion than express our admiration and thank you for the beautiful visions you have revealed to us from the Emerald Isle? We have delighted in listening to the tales of the fairies and elves, with which you have made us acquainted. We have been especially charmed by your poem about the little 'silver trout' ['The Song of Wandering Aengus'].

In his acceptance speech, Yeats paid tribute to the great Scandinavian literary tradition of Swedenborg, Ibsen and Bjørnson, and then laid the credit for his recognition at the feet of those involved in the Irish Literary Revival.

I owe much to those men, still more to those who
joined our movement a few years later, and when
I return to Ireland these men and women, now
growing old like myself, will see in this great honour
a fulfilment of that dream. I in my heart know how
little I might have deserved it if they had never existed.

When people wrote to congratulate him on the great honour
he had received, his stock reply was: 'I consider that this honour
has come to me less as an individual than as a representative of
Irish literature, it is part of Europe's welcome to the Free State.'

The early years of the decade had brought Yeats no fewer
than three honorary degrees from Irish and British universities
– the relatively badly schooled writer was now 'Dr Yeats',
several times over.

By 1925 Yeats had finished work on *A Vision*, based on the
revelations of George's automatic writing. He would have liked
to have been able to regard it as his magnum opus, but he wrote
to his publisher that 'I dare say I delude myself in thinking this
book my book of books'.

It was at around this time that his health began to deteriorate. He was almost half blind and hard of hearing. He had put on weight, he suffered from high blood pressure and was experiencing shortness of breath. In November 1924 he went to Italy with George, and when they returned to Ireland in February 1925 he threw himself into things with renewed vigour. He redoubled his efforts to have the Lane pictures returned to Dublin. (The art collector Hugh Lane had amassed an impressive collection of Impressionist paintings. He made a will leaving his collection to the National Gallery in London, but added a codicil just before his death in 1915 leaving the collection to Dublin. The codicil was unwitnessed and the British therefore ignored it.) Yeats was unsuccessful in his attempt to have the collection housed in Dublin but in 1959, some progress was made and a series of agreements now allow for the collection to be shared between London and Dublin.

In 1927, in his role as director of the Abbey Theatre he defended Sean O'Casey's *The Plough and the Stars* against the rioting audience. 'You have disgraced yourselves again,' he stated autocratically. 'Dublin has once more rocked the cradle of genius.'

In 1928 he found himself vainly battling the government's attempt to introduce strict censorship. He attended the Seanad to debate the Copyright Bill, but then retired to Ballylee to write.

That year, troubled by arthritis, influenza and an attack of the measles, Yeats began to feel his age. The aptly titled 'Death' gives an insight into his state of mind at that time.

> Nor dread nor hope attend
> A dying animal:
> A man awaits his end
> Dreading and hoping all;
> Many times he died,
> Many times rose again.
> A great man in his pride
> Confronting murderous men
> Casts derision upon
> Supersession of breath;
> He knows death to the bone –
> Man has created death.

George Yeats (left), Jean Hall, a friend (centre) and W.B. Yeats in *Yeats and Friends at Hotel Gardens Algeciras*, from a film reel discovered by eminent Yeats scholar Dr Ann Saddlemyer

In October he became seriously ill with congested lungs. The medical advice was lots of sunshine, so he and George travelled to Algeciras in November, where he continued to work. Once again, he contemplated death:

At Algeciras – A Meditation Upon Death

The heron-billed pale cattle-birds
That feed on some foul parasite
Of the Moroccan flocks and herds
Cross the narrow Straits to light
In the rich midnight of the garden trees
Till the dawn break upon those mingled seas.

Often at evening when a boy
Would I carry to a friend –
Hoping more substantial joy
Did an older mind commend –
Not such as are in Newton's metaphor,
But actual shells of Rosses' level shore.

Greater glory in the sun,
An evening chill upon the air,
Bid imagination run
Much on the Great Questioner;
What He can question, what if questioned I
Can with a fitting confidence reply.

Yeats at Rapallo
in 1929

His health continued to deteriorate and the Yeatses moved to the south of France where George thought her husband would get better medical care. He was prescribed bed rest and no work. They crossed the Italian border to Rapallo in February 1928, returning to Ireland the following April.

1928 was a difficult year for Yeats and for the Abbey, when it rejected Sean O'Casey's latest play *The Silver Tassie* and Yeats's correspondence on the matter was published in *The Times*. His blood pressure soared. George sold the Merrion Square house in May and they moved into a flat at 72 Fitzwilliam Square. He and George decided to winter in Rapallo, returning to Dublin in April. It was a fruitful time for his work – he said that writing had never come so easily to him and he wrote a poem to his old love, Olivia Shakespear.

After Long Silence

Speech after long silence; it is right,
All other lovers being estranged or dead,
Unfriendly lamplight hid under its shade,
The curtains drawn upon unfriendly night,
That we descant and yet again descant
Upon the supreme theme of Art and Song;
Bodily decrepitude is wisdom; young
We loved each other and were ignorant.

He and George continued to travel between Dublin and Rapallo, with a few stopovers in London, until 1931, when they rented a house in Killiney, overlooking the bay.

CHAPTER 16

Dreams of Death

*All that's beautiful
drifts away*

Ensconced in Killiney from February to May 1931, Yeats worked on a seven-volume edition of his collected works for his London publisher, Macmillan. In May he was awarded an honorary doctorate by Oxford University and he travelled there to have it conferred.

From late summer until May 1932, Yeats spent most of his time at Coole Park. Lady Gregory was dying and was glad of his company. While there, he worked on the establishment of an Irish Academy of Letters. Lady Gregory died on 23rd May, when Yeats was in Dublin on business. He later paid homage to his great friend and patron in 'The Municipal Gallery Revisited':

> Mancini's portrait of Augusta Gregory,
> 'Greatest since Rembrandt,' according to John Synge;
> A great ebullient portrait, certainly;
> But where is the brush that could show anything
> Of all that pride and humility?
> And I am in despair that time may bring
> Approved patterns of women or of men
> But not that selfsame excellence again.

Meanwhile, George had taken a lease on Yeats's final home, an 18th-century farmhouse with large gardens at Rathfarnham. They moved in in July. In September he launched the Irish Academy of Letters with himself as president. In October he sailed to America for his last lecture tour there, during which he promoted and raised funds for the new endeavour. He arrived back in Dublin in January 1933. Concerned that De Valera's government would cut the Abbey Theatre's subsidy, he had a meeting with him which reassured him about state support.

In the 1930s, Yeats flirted with Fascism and dabbled in eugenics, which was popular in upper-class circles at the time. He expressed his admiration for Mussolini and in 1933 he briefly became involved with the Blueshirts, the Irish Fascist organisation whose popularity was spreading throughout the country. In a letter to Olivia Shakespear he said:

> It is amusing to live in a country where men will always act. Where nobody is satisfied with thought … The chance of being shot is raising everybody's spirits enormously.

Yeats was accused of Nazism when he accepted the Goethe
Medal in 1934 – it was awarded by the city of Frankfurt, then
under Nazi control. However, he had little interest in Germany
and its politics (he had little interest in any country except
Ireland) but was an admirer of Goethe. Although his politics were
authoritarian and anti-democratic, he was not anti-Semitic.

Also in 1934, Yeats had a surgical procedure known as
the Steinach operation, which was, basically, a vasectomy. It
rejuvenated him psychologically and physically. His motivation
for undergoing the procedure was his perception that his sexual
energy had diminished. Afterwards he felt better physically and
began to write again enthusiastically (he had felt unable to write
in the aftermath of Lady Gregory's death). 'The Four Ages of
Man' included the lines

> He with body waged a fight
> But body won, it walks upright

He also became involved in numerous romantic liaisons.
He was very aware that he hadn't sown any wild oats during

his youth and seems to have wanted to make up the deficit. In autumn 1934 he met a 27-year-old actress, Margaret Ruddock, and became infatuated with her. He rented a flat in London and saw her whenever he was visiting the city. She wrote poetry and he encouraged her in this. In November he sent her a poem, never published, which recognised the May and September aspect of their relationship.

Margot

All famine struck sat I, and then
Those generous eyes on mine were cast,
Sat like other aged men
Dumbfounded, gazing on a past
That appeared constructed of
Lost opportunities to love.

O how can I that interest hold?
What offer to attentive eyes?
Mind grows young and body old;
When half-closed her eye-lid lies
A sort of hidden glory shall
About these stooping shoulders fall.

The Age of Miracles renew
Let me be loved as though still young
Or let me fancy that it's true
When my brief final years are gone
You shall have time to turn away
And cram those open eyes with day.

In December 1934 Yeats met the novelist Ethel Mannin. She was brilliant and engaging and Yeats was enthralled. He was able to conduct his affairs unhindered because George was concentrating her energies and attention on Anne and Michael, both teenagers. Even Yeats noticed that she had 'become a mother rather than a wife'.

In January 1935 he had an attack of lung congestion, a recurring problem for the rest of his life. By the spring he had regained his strength and agreed to undertake the editing of the *Oxford Book of Modern Verse* – as soon as it appeared, in November 1936, his selection of poets caused him to be ridiculed for his partisanship. The negative criticism gave an enormous boost to sales, so his publisher, at least, was happy.

Ethel Edith Mannin

In May 1935 Yeats was introduced to the poet Lady Dorothy Wellesley. He was impressed by her work and her social position (she had been married to the younger son of a Duke of Wellington), and her home in Sussex, where he had his own room.

In June 1935 Yeats celebrated his 70th birthday and was delighted by the extent to which he was feted. He looked back on his life in 'What Then?'

> His chosen comrades thought at school
> He must grow a famous man;
> He thought the same and lived by rule,
> All his twenties crammed with toil:
> *'What then?' sang Plato's ghost. 'What then?'*
>
> Everything he wrote was read,
> After certain years he won
> Sufficient money for his need,
> Friends that have been friends indeed;
> *'What then?' sang Plato's ghost. 'What then?*
>
> All his happier dreams came true –
> A small old house, wife, daughter, son,

Grounds where plum and cabbage grew,
Poets and Wits about him drew;
'What then?' sang Plato's ghost. 'What then?'

'The work is done,' grown old he thought,
'According to my boyish plan;
Let the fools rage, I swerved in naught,
Something to perfection brought';
But louder sang that ghost, 'What then?

In the same year he was offered a Harvard professorship,
on the condition that he would be in residence there. Lucrative
though it was, he turned down the invitation in favour of
wintering in Majorca for the good of his health.

During these years his friends were beginning to die. He had
anticipated this in 'The Old Men Admiring Themselves in the
Water', published when he was in his late 30s.

I heard the old, old men say,
'Everything alters
And one by one we drop away.'
They had hands like claws, and their knees

Were twisted like the old thorn-trees
By the waters.
I heard the old, old men say,
'All that's beautiful drifts away
Like the waters.'

Settled in Palma for the winter, he became ill with nephritis and asked George to come out to Majorca to look after him. She stayed in Majorca with him for three months, then returned to Dublin. Yeats followed her later that year, travelling via London and staying in Sussex with Dorothy Wellesley for some time.

1937 was a notable year for Yeats. London's Athenaeum Club offered him membership on the grounds of his literary distinction. In March he went to London to prepare for a series of BBC broadcasts and he met Edith Shackleton, his last and probably most important love. She was 53, a retired unmarried journalist with a house in West Sussex, The Chantry House, which she shared with her sister. Yeats had his own room there and spent a lot of time in Sussex, writing prolifically. He also rented rooms in Holland Park in London, so that he could be with Edith when he had to be in the city.

In winter 1937 Yeats had the idea that he would like to take advantage of a better climate – this time in Monte Carlo, with Edith. He set sail on 6 January 1938. In March Edith was replaced at Yeats's side by George – the two most important women in Yeats's life seem to have reached an accommodation. At the end of March he travelled to England and stayed at the Chantry House with Edith for six weeks. He worked solidly while there, finishing his last play, *Purgatory*, and dreaming dreams of death.

He returned to Ireland in May to attend to some business for the Abbey Theatre and the Cuala Press, then went back to Edith in July. He had written to her:

> I do not want henceforth to be away from you for any
> length of time.

He was back in Dublin on 10 August for the opening night of *Purgatory*. It was the last time he appeared in public in his native city. In October he heard that Olivia Shakespear had died. He was now growing frail, but despite this he went to stay

W.B. Yeats and Dorothy Violet Wellesley (née Ashton), Duchess of Wellington with Edith later that month. George met him in London at the end of November and they travelled together to Cap-Martin on the French Riviera. Edith was to join them at the end of January 1939.

Yeats was in good health for the first weeks of his stay in France but in the last days of January his health began to deteriorate rapidly. Edith arrived on the 28th, just in time to sit with him as he died. That morning, he had been able to sit up and had made some corrections to his final poem, 'The Black Tower'. The last verse reads:

> There in the tomb the dark grows blacker,
> But wind comes up from the shore:
> They shake when the winds roar,
> Old bones upon the mountain shake.

CHAPTER 17

Aftermath

Statue of Yeats in Sligo

Plant me in Sligo

Before he died, Yeats told George to 'bury me up there [the cemetery at Roquebrune] and then in a year's time when the newspapers have forgotten me, dig me up and plant me in Sligo'. At the time of his death the situation in Europe was so unstable and uncertain that George had no option but to have him buried in France, in the cemetery at Roquebrune. It was almost 10 years before his final wishes could be fully honoured.

Yeats's first burial was attended by a few friends, but George was the only member of the family present. She took a 10-year renewable lease on the grave at Roquebrune (this was normal practice in France) and intended to have her husband disinterred and moved to Ireland at the earliest opportunity. However, the Second World War intervened and it was 1948 before plans could be made to organise the removal and reburial. In an interesting twist of fate, Seán MacBride, the son of Maud Gonne and John MacBride, was the Irish Minister for External Affairs at the time, and it fell to him to

Seán MacBride

French military guard of honour for Yeats's coffin

The *LÉ Macha* pulls away from Nice harbour

organise the repatriation of Yeats's remains. The poet was to receive a state funeral.

However, at some point during the war Yeats's body and that of the Englishman in the neighbouring grave were dug up and reburied in a different location in Roquebrune cemetery. Neither family had been notified, so this caused some consternation and confusion when arrangements were made in September 1948 to bring Yeats's remains to Sligo. However, Yeats family members were satisfied that it was Yeats's body that was transferred to a new coffin.

The coffin had a French military guard of honour for its journey on 6 September from the cemetery to the harbour at Villefranche, where it was transferred, with a lot of pomp, to *LÉ Macha*, a corvette in the Irish Naval Service. The military guard presented arms and the French and Irish national anthems were played as the coffin was brought on board and tied down to the deck. The *Macha* docked at Galway harbour on 17 September, where it was met by a guard of honour, with George, Anne, Michael and Jack Yeats in attendance. The

coffin was carried in a procession through the city of Galway en route to Mayo and Sligo and people lined the road to pay their respects.

When the procession arrived in Sligo it was met by the mayor, Michael Rooney, who made a speech paying 'sincere tribute to the memory of one whose genius was inspired by the lakes and mountains of our countryside, and whose poetry has given the name of Sligo a place in the literature of the world.'

The day was dreary, and Ben Bulben was shrouded in mist when the cortège arrived at Drumcliffe churchyard, which was crowded with the great and the good, including Eamon De Valera and Lord Longford, a bishop and five other clergymen. The ritual was performed, the

Yeats' coffin is blessed

prayers were said and the gravediggers covered the coffin with the clay of Sligo.

In his poem 'Under Ben Bulben', written the year before his death, Yeats had been very specific about his final resting place:

> Under bare Ben Bulben's head
> In Drumcliff churchyard Yeats is laid.
> An ancestor was rector there
> Long years ago, a church stands near,
> By the road an ancient cross.
> No marble, no conventional phrase;
> On limestone quarried near the spot
> By his command these words are cut:
>
> > *Cast a cold eye*
> > *On life, on death.*
> > *Horseman, pass by.*

When his simple limestone headstone was erected it bore the last three lines of the poem.

When Yeats had made his burial wishes known, his sister Lily had objected, on the ground that no Yeats since the 18th century had had a tombstone. She didn't understand why he was breaking with family tradition. The tourists and scholars who make the pilgrimage to his grave under Ben Bulben are glad that he did.

Select Bibliography

1865   William Butler Yeats is born in Dublin on 13 June.

1867   The Yeats family moves to London.

1872   The family moves to Sligo.

1874   The family returns to London.

1877   Yeats is enrolled in the Godolphin School, London.

1881   The family returns to Dublin; Yeats attends the Erasmus Smith High School.

1884   Yeats is enrolled in the Dublin Metropolitan School of Art; meets George 'AE' Russell.

1885   The Dublin Hermetic Society convenes for the first time. Yeats's first works are published in the *Dublin University Review*. He meets John O'Leary and Katharine Tynan.

1887   The family moves back to London; Yeats meets Madame Blavatsky, founder of the Theosophical Society.

1888   Yeats joins the Esoteric Section of the Theosophical Society.
Fairy and Folk Tales of the Irish Peasantry

1889   On 30 January Yeats meets Maud Gonne for the first time.
The Wanderings of Oisin and Other Poems

1890   The Rhymers' Club is founded; Yeats joins the Order of
the Golden Dawn and is asked to resign from the
Theosophical Society.

1891   Yeats proposes to Maud Gonne.
John Sherman

1892   *The Countess Cathleen*
Irish Fairy Tales

1893   *The Celtic Twilight*

1895   Yeats edits *A Book of Irish Verse*.

1896   Yeats meets Lady Gregory; he begins an affair with Olivia
Shakespear.
Rosa Alchemica

1897 Yeats ends his affair with Olivia Shakespear.
The Tables of the Law
The Adoration of the Magi
The Secret Rose

1899 *The Countess Cathleen* is staged at the Antient Concert
Rooms in Dublin; the Irish Literary Theatre is opened.
The Wind Among the Reeds

1900 *The Shadowy Waters*

1901 *Diarmuid and Grania* is staged in Dublin.

1902 Yeats meets James Joyce; *Cathleen Ni Houlihan* is staged
in Dublin.
Where There is Nothing

1903 Maud Gonne marries John MacBride on 21 February;
Yeats goes to the US on a lecture tour.
Ideas of Good and Evil
In the Seven Woods
The Hour-Glass

1904 *The Shadowy Waters* plays in Dublin and *Where There is Nothing* is stage in London; On 27 December the Abbey Theatre opens with, among other plays, *On Baile's Strand*.
The King's Threshold

1905 Maud Gonne gets a legal separation; the Abbey goes on a British tour.
Stories of Red Hanrahan

1906 *Poems 1899–1905*

1907 J. M. Synge's *The Playboy of the Western World* is greeted with riots at the Abbey; John B. Yeats moves to New York; *The Unicorn from the Stars* plays at the Abbey.
Deirdre

1908 Yeats has an affair with Mabel Dickinson; the Cuala Press is founded.
Collected Works in Verse and Prose (eight volumes)

1910 Yeats is awarded a Civil List pension of £150 per annum; the main Abbey benefactor withdraws her support when the theatre refuses to close after the death of Edward VII.
The Green Helmet and Other Poems

1911   The Abbey goes on a tour of the US.
Synge and the Ireland of his Time
Plays for an Irish Theatre

1912   *The Cutting of an Agate*

1913   *Poems Written in Discouragement*

1914   Yeats goes on a four-month lecture tour of the US;
war in Europe.
Responsibilities

1915   Yeats turns down a knighthood.

1916   Easter Rising begins on 24 April; the leaders, including
John MacBride, are executed in May; Yeats proposes to
Maud Gonne.
Reveries over Childhood and Youth

1917   Yeats buys Thoor Ballylee; proposes to Iseult Gonne;
marries Georgie Hyde-Lees on 20 October.
The Wild Swans at Coole

1918   First World War ends on 11 November.
Per Amica Silentia Lunae

1919 Irish War of Independence begins; Anne Yeats is born on
26 February.
Two Plays for Dancers

1920 Yeats goes on five-month lecture tour of US.

1921 Michael Yeats is born on 22 August; Anglo–Irish Treaty
signed on 6 December.
Michael Robartes and the Dancer
Four Plays for Dancers
Four Years

1922 John B. Yeats dies in New York on 3 February; Yeats is
nominated to Seanad Éireann; Irish Civil War begins
in June.
The Trembling of the Veil
Later Poems
Plays in Prose and Verse

1923 Civil War ends in May; Yeats is awarded Nobel Prize for
Literature in November.
Plays and Controversies

1924 *Essays*
The Cat and the Moon and Certain Poems

1925 *The Bounty of Sweden*
Early Poems and Stories
A Vision (private publication)

1926 *Estrangement*
Autobiographies

1927 *October Blast*

1928 Yeats resigns from the Seanad.
The Tower
Sophocles' King Oedipus
The Death of Synge

1929 *The Winding Stair*
A Packet for Ezra Pound

1930 *The Words upon the Window Pane* opens at the Abbey on 17 November.

1931 Yeats is awarded an honorary degree by Oxford University.

1932   Lady Gregory dies on 22 May; Yeats and George move to Rathfarnham in Dublin; in November Yeats embarks on a four-month US lecture tour.
Stories of Michael Robartes and His Friends
Words for Music Perhaps

1933   *The Winding Stair and Other Poems*
The Collected Poems of W. B. Yeats

1934   Yeats elects to have the Steinach operation in April.
Letters to the New Island
Wheels and Butterflies
The Collected Plays of W. B. Yeats
The King of the Great Clock Tower

1935   George Russell dies on 17 July.
A Full Moon in March
Dramatis Personae

1936   *The Oxford Book of Modern Verse* (ed.)

1937   *A Vision* (revised)
Essays, 1931–1936

1938   Yeats attends the opening of *Purgatory* at the Abbey on 10 August; Olivia Shakespear dies in October.
The Herne's Egg
New Poems

1939   Yeats dies on 28 January and is buried at Roquebrune in France.
Last Poems and Two Plays
On the Boiler

1940   *Last Poems and Plays*

1941   Yeats's body is brought from France and reburied in Drumcliffe churchyard in Sligo.

Index to Poems Cited

After Long Silence **211**
Among School Children **183**
At Algeciras – A Meditation Upon Death **208**

Black Tower, The **228**

Coat, The **126**
Coole Park and Ballylee, 1931 **167**
Coole Park, 1929 **142**

Death **206**

Easter 1916 **177**
Ephemera **50**

Fiddler of Dooney, The **154**
Four Ages of Man, The **218**

Grey Rock, The **49**

He Thinks of Those Who Have Spoken Evil of His Beloved **78**
He Wishes for the Cloths of Heaven **52**

In Memory of Eva Gore-Booth and Con Markiewicz **150**
In Memory of Your Dreams One July Night **75**
Into the Twilight **107**
Irish Airman Foresees His Death, An **139**

Lake Isle of Inisfree, The **54**
Love and Death **41**
Lover Mourns for the Loss of Love, The **90**

Margot **220**
Municipal Gallery Revisited **211**

No Second Troy **88**

Old Men Admiring Themselves in the Water, The **224**

Pardon Old Fathers **92**

Prayer For My Daughter, A **100**
Prayer For My Son, A **101**
Prayer on Going into My House, A **162**

Road at My Door, The **187**

Second Coming, The **199**
Secret Rose, The **66**
Sixteen Dead Men **177**
Song of Wandering Aengus, The **153**
Song, A **82**
Stolen Child, The **155**

To a Child Dancing in the Wind **31**
To Be Carved on a Stone at Thoor Ballylee **165**

Under Ben Bulben **237**

What Then? **223**
When You Are Old **75**
Wild Swans at Coole, The **135**

Select Bibliography

Arnold, Bruce, *Jack Yeats*. New Haven and London: Yale University Press, 1988.

Collected Poems of W. B. Yeats. London: Macmillan, second edition, 1959.

Howes, Marjorie and Kelly, John (eds.), *The Cambridge Companion to W. B. Yeats*. Cambridge: CUP, 2006.

Jeffares, Norman A., *W. B. Yeats – A New Biography*. London and New York: Continuum, revised edition, 2001.

Lyons, F. S. L., *Ireland Since the Famine*. London: Weidenfeld and Nicolson, 1971.

Maddox, Brenda, *George's Ghosts – A New Life of W. B. Yeats*. London: Picador, 1999.

Picture credits

The publisher gratefully acknowledges the following image copyright holders. All images are copyright © individual rights holders unless stated otherwise. Every effort has been made to trace copyright holders, or copyright holders not mentioned here. If there have been any errors or omissions, the publisher would be happy to rectify this in any reprint.